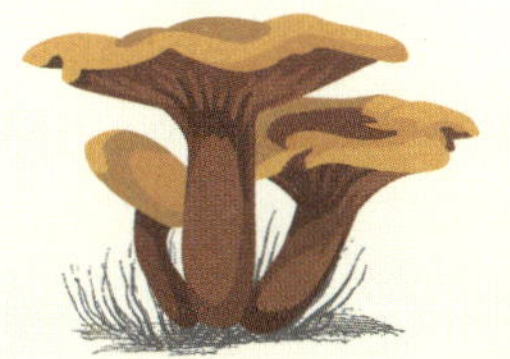

MUSHROOMS

20 MODERN PAINT-BY-NUMBER PRINTS

DAVID TRAWIN AND A. K. ROXAS

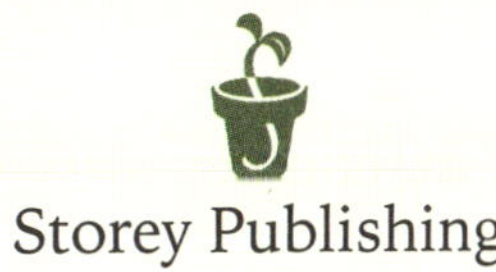

Storey Publishing

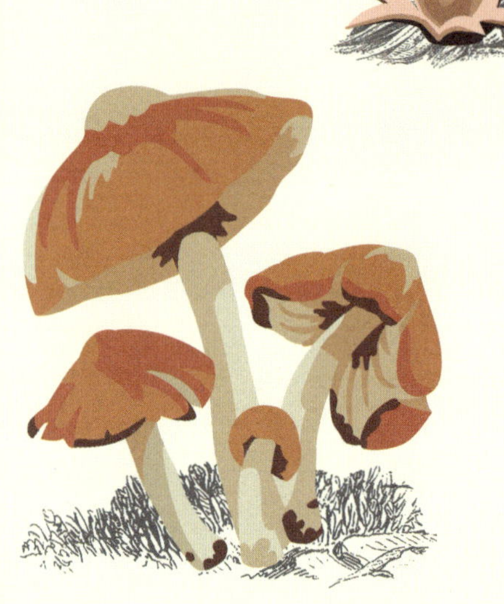
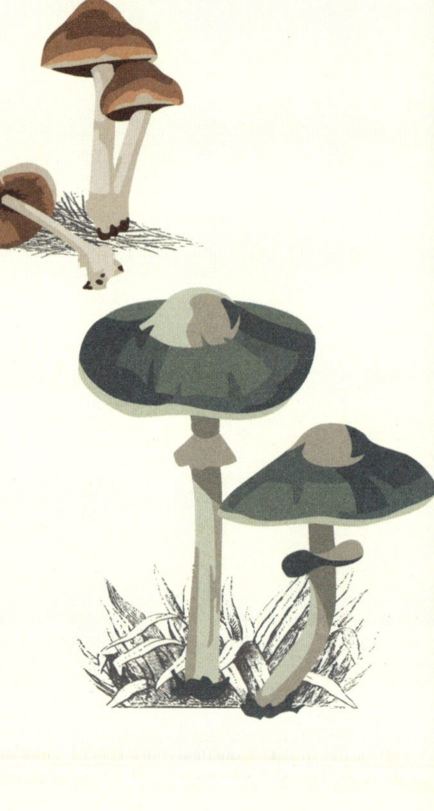

CONTENTS

THE 20 MUSHROOMS

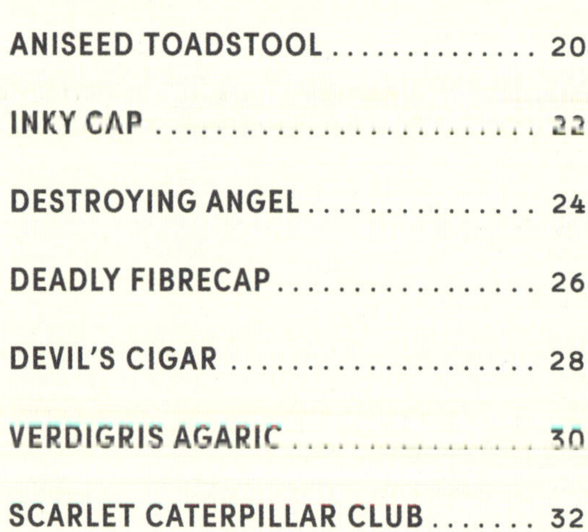
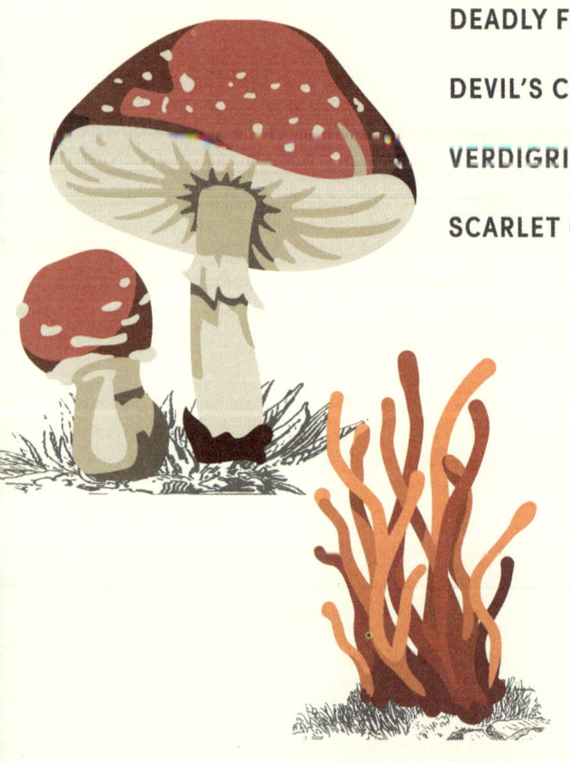
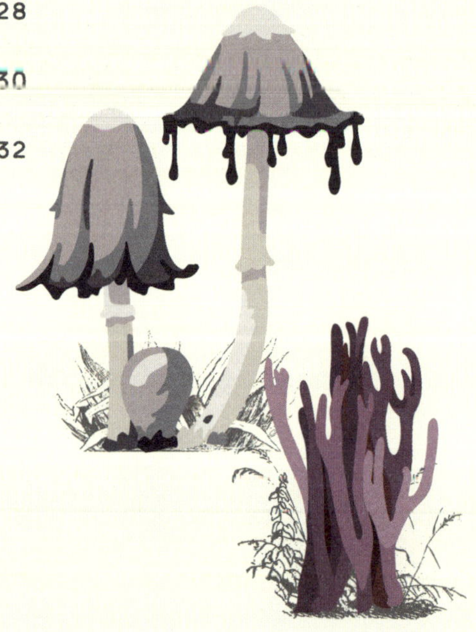

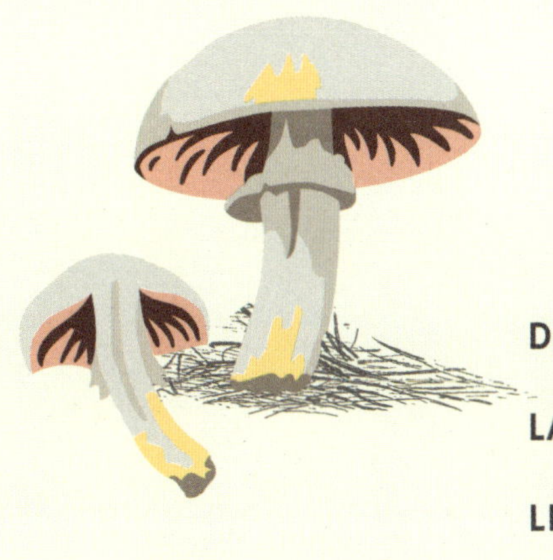

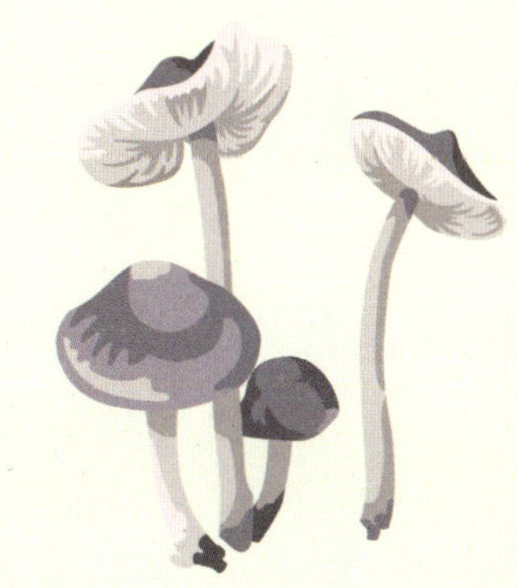

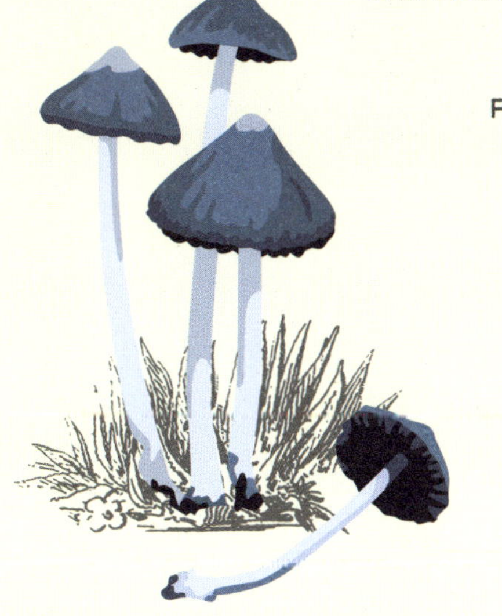

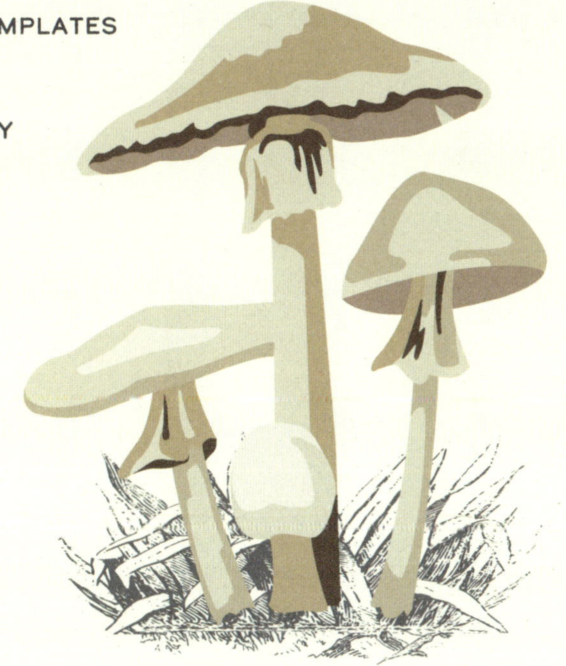

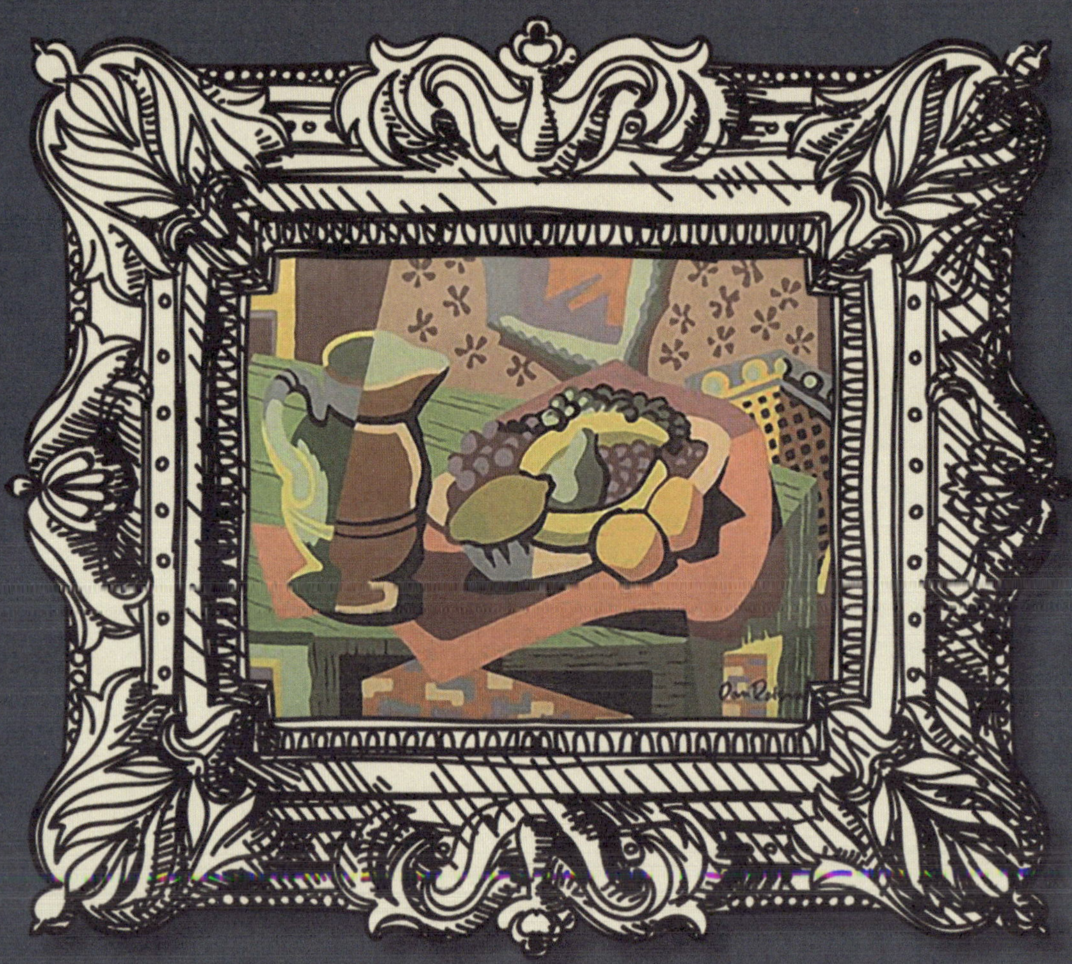

ABSTRACT NO. 1

This was the first paint-by-number kit, made by Dan Robbins in 1950, which kicked off an entire genre of DIY art.

I DIDN'T CREATE THE CONCEPT OF PAINT BY NUMBER

That distinction goes to Dan Robbins, a packaging designer who worked at Palmer Show Card Paint Company in the 1950s. He based the idea on a clever teaching style Leonardo da Vinci employed. According to Robbins, da Vinci would "hand out numbered patterns indicating where certain colors should be used in specific projects" to his apprentices.

Robbins took that idea and updated it to appeal to the hobby-loving postwar generation, and paint by number was born. The original sets were called Craft Master kits and launched in 1951. Twenty million sets were sold in 1955 alone. They were so popular that everyone from White House officials to Andy Warhol got in on the game. Search online for Warhol's *Do It Yourself* series from 1962 if you want to check out his cheeky take.

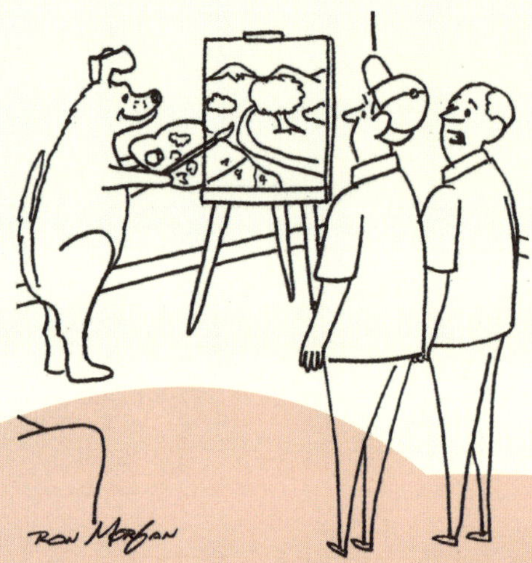

"What's so amazing? It's a paint-by-the-numbers
artist kit."

GATEKEEPING ART

Of course, anything popular draws its critics. Some criticized the kits for not being "real art," with the magazine *American Artist* proclaiming, "I don't know what America is coming to, when thousands of people, many of them adults, are willing to be regimented into brushing paint on a jig-saw miscellany of dictated shapes and all by rote. Can't you rescue some of these souls?" Oh, if that mid-century art snob could see us now.

Today we have emojis, avatars, AI-generated images, and NFTs. We have Instagram, Etsy, affordable art shows, street art, and murals on every corner. We use images in place of language, as social currency, to influence, self-identify, motivate, and activate. We live in a much more aesthetically aware society with infinite access to prints, posters, and reproductions. Art is everywhere and aesthetics can be enjoyed no matter what form the art comes in.

THE NEXT WAVE OF
PAINT BY NUMBER

The Craft Master kits re-created classical painting themes, reproduced old masters, and laid the foundation for bringing the art experience to the masses. But the boundaries of paint by number are ripe for expansion. And that's where this book comes in.

I want to explore what happens when these ready-made pieces come closer to graphic design. What can it look like when we combine elements of pop culture, typography, pixel art, absurdist, punk, street culture, and other newer art movements?

These are all fertile grounds for exploration.

I WANT US TO THINK
OF ART AS MOVEABLE.
IMMERSIVE.

I grew up admiring graphics on skateboards, combing through my brother's *Thrasher* magazine, and making punk zines and later was a follower and participant in the scene around *Juxtapoz* magazine.

I believe that art should be accessible and that every piece doesn't need to be treated as preciously as the *Mona Lisa*. Some art can be ephemeral. It can exist just to capture a feeling of that time and place, even if it's just half a second.

And I want us to be haphazard with it. Move it around. Swap it in and out. Hang and rehang it in our homes to give us a renewed sense of our surroundings.

Robbins himself said of paint by number, "It is the experience of art, and it brings that experience to the individual who would normally not pick up a brush, not dip it in paint." And that's what I want to do. Bring that experience to you.

So let's pick up a brush. Dip it in paint.

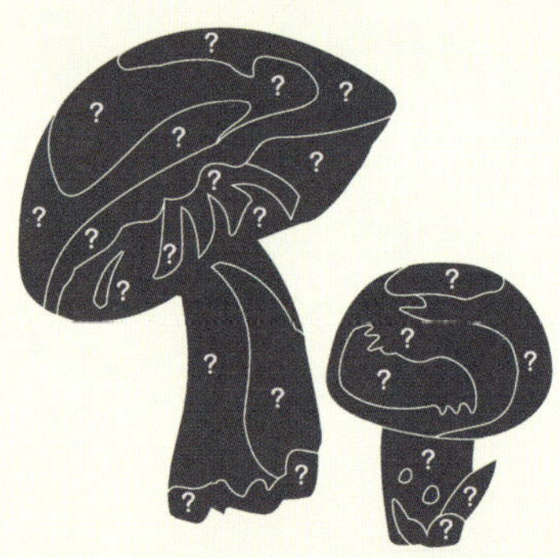

WHY MUSHROOMS?

Because they are unlike anything else in nature. They're bizarre, deadly, mysterious, bold, and attention seeking. Some are unexpectedly benign while others are poised to kill. I want to upend your perception of these inconspicuous powerhouses with otherworldly shapes and colors and facts about their curious abilities.

For instance, did you know the iconic red and white-polka-dotted mushroom from Super Mario Bros. is called the *Amanita muscaria* (see Fly Agaric on page 18) and would take Mario out faster than Bowser's goons could? Or that the disconcerting radiantly blue *Entoloma hochstetteri* (see Sky-Blue Mushroom on page 44) looks like it screams, "Killing is fun," but nope, it's completely benign though unpalatable.

I've selected 20 mushrooms that are chameleons, healers, killers, delicacies, or just plain pretty. You'll have two options for which template you want to paint: the light-colored background or the dark-colored one. And once you're done, you can frame it, hang it, gift it, or just admire your handiwork.

HOW TO PAINT BY NUMBER

"Perfect" is often confused with mechanical precision, but the best-looking work comes from confidence in your brushstrokes. There is not one but thousands of brilliant outcomes.

There's no single "right" way to paint. Some people prefer clean, crisp lines, some like more organic applications of color with looser boundaries, and some prefer chaos and lean into bold abstraction.

MAKING ART CAN BE INSPIRING, RESTORATIVE, TRANSCENDENT, AND CALMING . . . IF YOU LET IT BE.

The paint-by-number templates are just that, templates to help you understand the overall pattern and colors needed to achieve the image shown in the art reference. The most important thing is just giving yourself the creative space to play.

We'll cover the basics of getting paint on paper, and once you're comfortable there, feel free to experiment with your tools and techniques. I would recommend acrylic paint for these templates, as it will be the most opaque, covering up the lines and numbers, and will likely offer the closest color match to what you see in the example.

WHAT YOU NEED

- At minimum, 2 brushes—a small round #3 and a small flat #4. I recommend Princeton brushes, but the acrylic Artist's Loft brushes work, too.

- Acrylic paint—each color recipe will specify the paint color and amount you need. To complete every mushroom template in the book, I recommend Liquitex Basics 48-piece set, but most acrylic paint sets include a selection of the primary colors you'll need. (We'll get into color mixing later.)

- Glass jar—for water to rinse your brushes. Any random vessel will do. I've used a leftover jelly jar, an old coffee mug, or even just a plastic cup.

If you'd prefer to use other coloring materials, feel free to try markers, colored pencils, or pastels. The most important thing is to pick a medium with a wide color range and swatch the colors (see page 99), so you can get the closest color match. The final effect will be slightly different from the example image, but the overall experience of creating art will still be there.

I recommend Prismacolor pencils or markers, which you can find at most art stores and online. However, these will be more transparent, so you'll likely see the underlying lines and numbers from the templates.

This is just where to start. Where you end up is totally up to you.

USING READY-MADE COLORS

Most art or craft stores have an array of premixed paint colors. They won't have the exact colors shown in the book (that's what the color recipes starting on page 99 are for), but you should be able to find a close match as long as their shade range is large enough. Just make sure they're acrylic paints, and I'd suggest a matte finish. If you're looking to get painting without wading through the nuances of color mixing and matching, you can buy the premade color palette for each mushroom from coloready.com/mushroomcollection.

WHERE TO SHOP FOR SUPPLIES

Depending on where you live, I'd recommend a local art store (#shopsmall). Otherwise, check out online art suppliers. The paint and brush brands I recommend will give you the most ideal outcome, but go with what you can find and afford.

USING AND TESTING THE COLOR RECIPES

Accompanying each swatch, you'll find simple recipes for mixing the suggested colors for each mushroom. The recipes list the approximate ratios or parts of each color's ingredients to get you as close as possible to the color you see in the corresponding swatch. I recommend using a 1 mL oral syringe, but you can use anything small (a single drop, a ¼ teaspoon, one squeeze of a pipet) as long as you use a consistent measurement tool. I'd just suggest going with the smallest measurement tool, so you don't waste any paint.

Of course, there's nothing wrong with freestyling and finding your own color combinations if you want to get creative.

HOW TO MIX PAINT

First off, I want to say: don't be intimidated. This is truly more an art than a science, but the Paint Swatch recipes should hopefully make this feel straightforward. It can be a messy process (hence, the paper towels in the supply list), and at first you might feel like it's impossible to match the color, but once you see it finally coming together it will feel so satisfying.

PAINT MIXING SUPPLIES

- Palette pad or paper plate (for mixing colors)
- A palette knife (to mix colors)
- A cup of water (for cleaning palette knife)
- Paper towels (for general cleanup)

To create a color from a Paint Swatch recipe, measure the paints into one pile on your palette pad. Use your palette knife to flatten that pile. Move the paint back and forth, scrape it off, slap it down, beat it up a bit. Do this until it's thoroughly mixed and you no longer see any of the individual colors.

Test your color by painting a dab beside each swatch in the blank spot provided on the Paint Swatch Key. If the color is too dull, try adding a pinch of the most vibrant color (e.g., the brightest color) in that recipe. If it's too light, try adding Neutral Gray 5 or Ivory Black to darken. If it's too dark, try adding Titanium White or Unbleached Titanium to it. These should be small tweaks as the color recipe will get you very close to the intended color.

POINTERS ON THE PROPERTIES OF PAINT

- It takes much less of a dark color to tint your paint than it does of a light color.

- Paints dry a tiny bit darker than they appear when they're wet.

- Mix in some water to your paint if it is starting to thicken during the course of your work. If you want to save your paint for a short period, apply a sheet of plastic wrap directly on the paint, tightening to leave no space for air.

HOW TO STORE YOUR PAINTS

Store the paints away from direct sunlight and any extreme temperatures. The ideal environment is room temperature, with the caps closed so the paints don't dry out. If you find your paints have gotten a little too thick from sitting, you can always add a bit of water to help thin them out.

LOAD YOUR BRUSH

The same brush can be used to paint fine details or fill in large areas; it all depends on how you load your brush (meaning how you dip it in the paint). The key is to load it proportionately to the area you're looking to paint. That might take some practice, so until you feel like you understand this technique, it never hurts to follow the adage "less is more." You can always reload your brush to continue painting, but too much paint can make working in smaller areas unmanageable. You'll be surprised how little paint you'll need on the tip of your brush to paint tight corners, but play with this to get a feel for it.

It likely doesn't need to be said, but I'll say it anyway. The numbers on the template correspond to the numbered paint colors shown for each mushroom on the Paint Swatch Key. So once you've got your paints mixed and your brush loaded with color, paint the corresponding numbers on the template.

If you want to practice before jumping right in, feel free to draw various small shapes on your own paper, and practice loading your brush and filling in the shapes. For example, you can draw a 2-inch-tall Washington Monument, and paint it to get a feel for how to paint in small spaces.

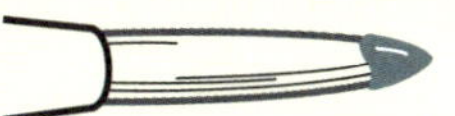

Small Details

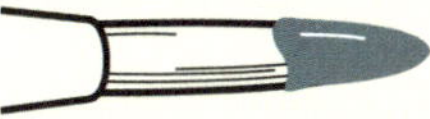

Mid-Size Areas

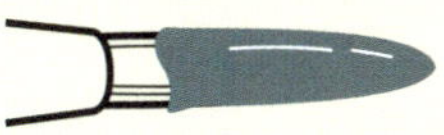

Large Areas

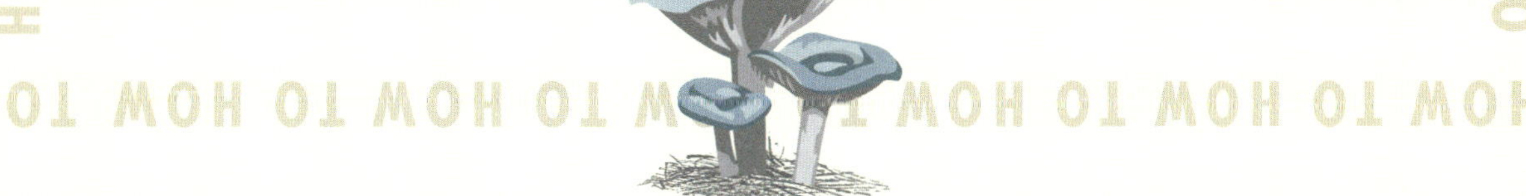

PAINT LIGHT TO DARK

If you need to make corrections, it's easier to cover light paint with dark, so it's generally a best practice to work from light to dark.

WASH AND REPOINT YOUR BRUSH

The texture of the paint on your brush can start to thicken and become difficult to work with after a while, so make sure to wash your brush every few minutes to start fresh. Dry it off with a paper towel (gently, not with the full force Bob Ross used to dry his brushes). After drying, be sure to repoint your brush by pinching the tip and shaping it to a crisp point. This will give you the most accurate results. Wash, dry, and point your brush when you're finished working to keep your brushes healthier longer.

FOLLOW THE CONTOURS

Paint along the contours of each segment so the subtle paint texture reinforces the direction of each shape.

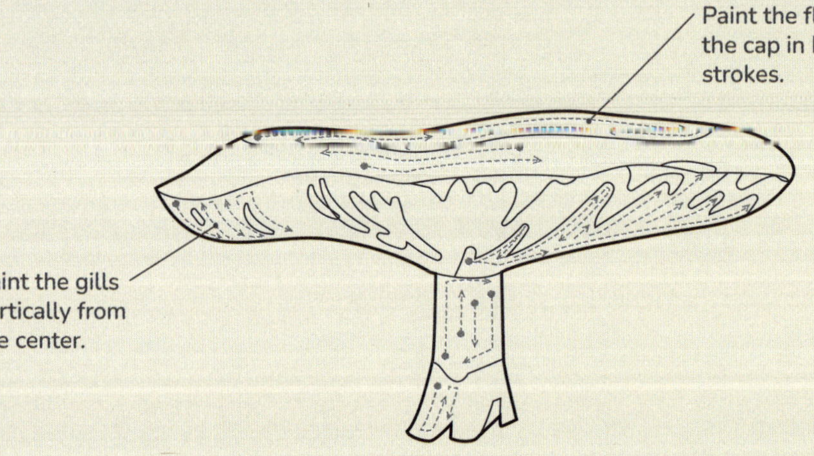

SO, YOU'RE ALL DONE . . . NOW WHAT?

The finished paintings from this book are intended to be displayed. These are not meant to be handled with white gloves but to give you good-looking, practical art to decorate and redecorate with. Plus you can have the sweet satisfaction of knowing you created a piece of art, imperfectly perfect as it is.

20 IDEAS FOR DISPLAYING YOUR FINISHED PAINTING

1. Hang it up in a prominent spot in your living room so that the next time someone comes over you can say, "See that? I painted it." Make sure you take all the credit.

2. Give it to your mom, grandma, or friend who is hard to shop for, a coworker you need a favor from, or that dude who lives next door who's always incredibly nice to you. Tell them you painted it just for them even though it's not true.

3. Cut out the painted mushrooms and make collages with them. Feel incredibly artsy.

4. Hang them as part of a gallery wall, mixed in with other paintings, embroidery pieces, or objects. Talk loudly about how you painted some of the pieces at your next dinner party.

5. When you go to Ikea to get frames (they carry the perfect size for these pages), be sure to tell everyone within earshot about how you need frames for the art you just painted.

6. Pushpin some on a corkboard in your office, so that on your next Zoom call, when someone compliments you on your background, you can say, "Oh, that? I painted it."

7. Mount three on foam core and hang them up in a horizontal space. Pretend you're a gallery.

8. Scan your painting and blow up the size to make a huge print. You can then get this printed out at your local office supply store, and you'll have a giant piece of very affordable art.

9. Hang up the colorful ones in a woodland-themed kid's room. Tell everyone that all the art was made by you.

10. Hang it up in your powder room, so the next time someone needs to pee, you can yell through the door that you painted the painting they're staring at.

11. Hang it up in your bedroom so that you can tell whoever might be sleeping with you that night that you painted that.

12. Give it to your best friend after a big fight. Say, "I painted this for me, but you can have it."

13. Give it to your sister who tells you that you never give her anything good. Remind her that you painted it every time you go over to her house.

14. Leave one lying on your coffee table or dining table the next time someone comes over. Move it quickly and say, "Oh, sorry, that's just something I've been working on."

15. Hang one at your brother's house when he's not home. See how long it takes for him to notice.

16. Gift one to your kid or niece/nephew for their birthday or a holiday. Tell them that they won't appreciate the thing they actually wanted as much as they'll appreciate this.

17. Take a picture of it and get it tattooed on you.

18. Let your kid or niece/nephew turn it in as their art project, and be known forever as the cool parent or aunt/uncle.

19. Go to your local hardware store, buy a miter saw, and make custom frames for your paintings so that you can tell everyone you painted *and* framed them yourself. (Overachiever.)

20. Confidently tell everyone about each fact you learned—like how the fly agaric is poisonous but the black trumpet isn't. Feel like a mushroom expert. (Just be sure to change the subject when answering the questions requires real substance.)

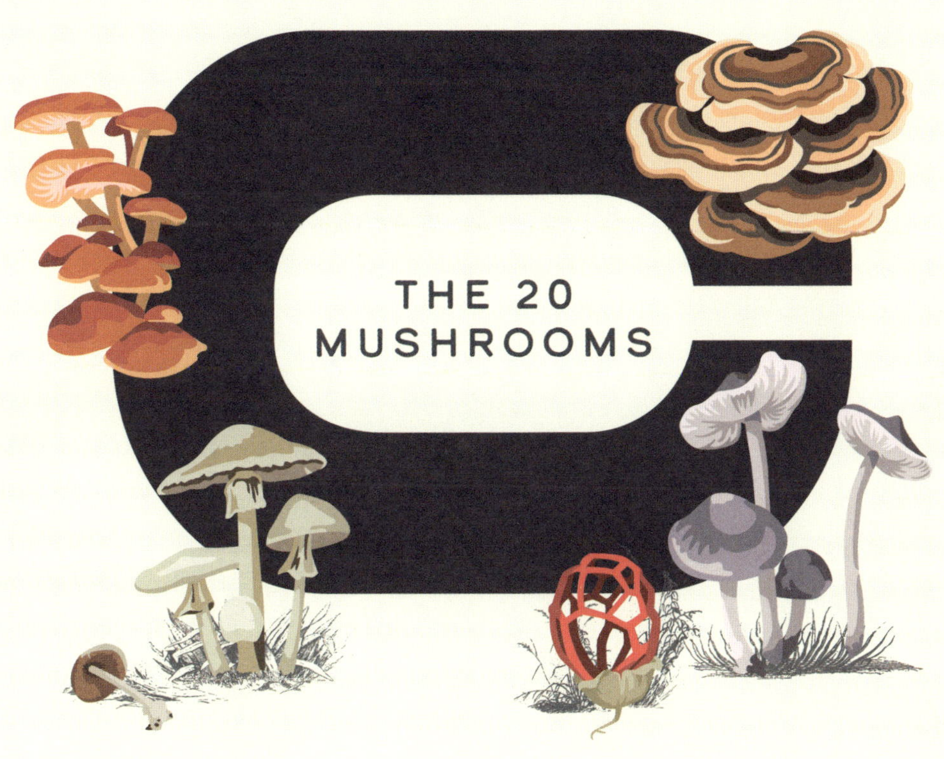

THE 20 MUSHROOMS

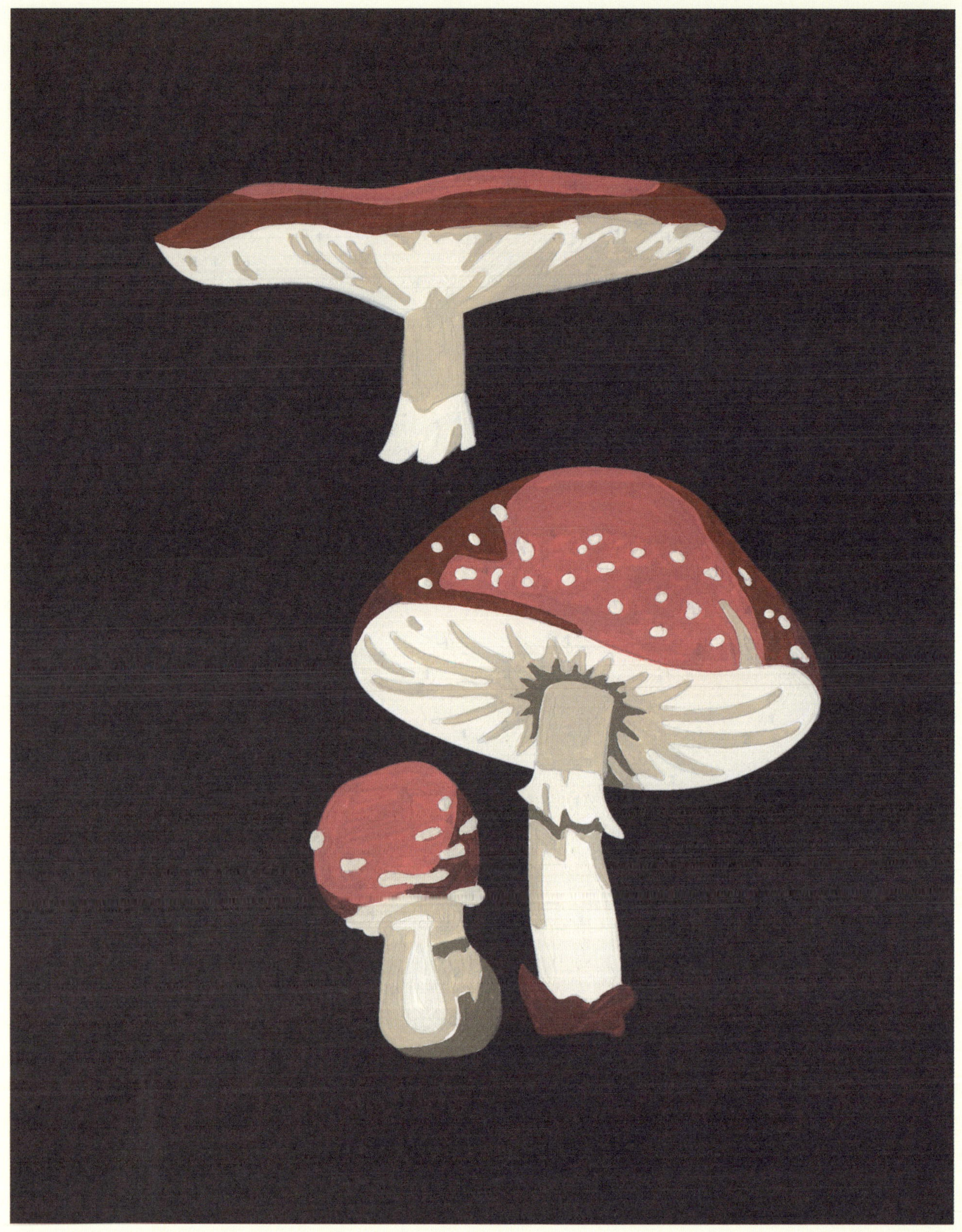

FLY AGARIC

Amanita muscaria

FLY AGARIC

AMANITA MUSCARIA

THE ONE EVERYBODY THINKS THEY KNOW

When you picture a 'shroom, you might be picturing an *Amanita muscaria*. It has a signature red cap with white spots that is similar to the mushrooms you've likely seen in fairytales, video games, cartoons, stickers, those black-light psychedelic posters, and more. In fact, the fly agaric is pretty pivotal in *Alice's Adventures in Wonderland*. Alice finds a caterpillar sitting on this 'shroom and it tells her to eat one side if she wants to grow huge or the other side if she wants to shrink.

But don't eat it if you're not Alice. It's a poisonous fungus that was once used as a pesticide. People would crumble up the caps and place them in saucers of milk. It would attract flies (hence the name) and boom, dead. It has hallucinogenic properties that are different from psilocybin, but it can also cause unsavory symptoms like stomach cramps or making you poop your pants. (Don't ask how I know.)

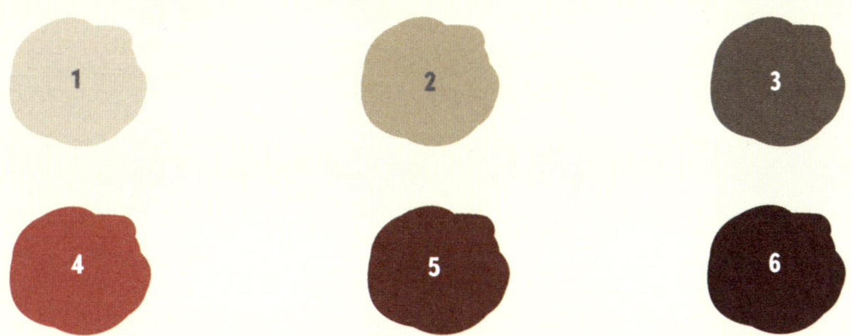

TO BLEND YOUR OWN COLORS FOR THIS PRINT, SEE PAGE 99 FOR BLENDING RECIPES AND SWATCH SAMPLES.

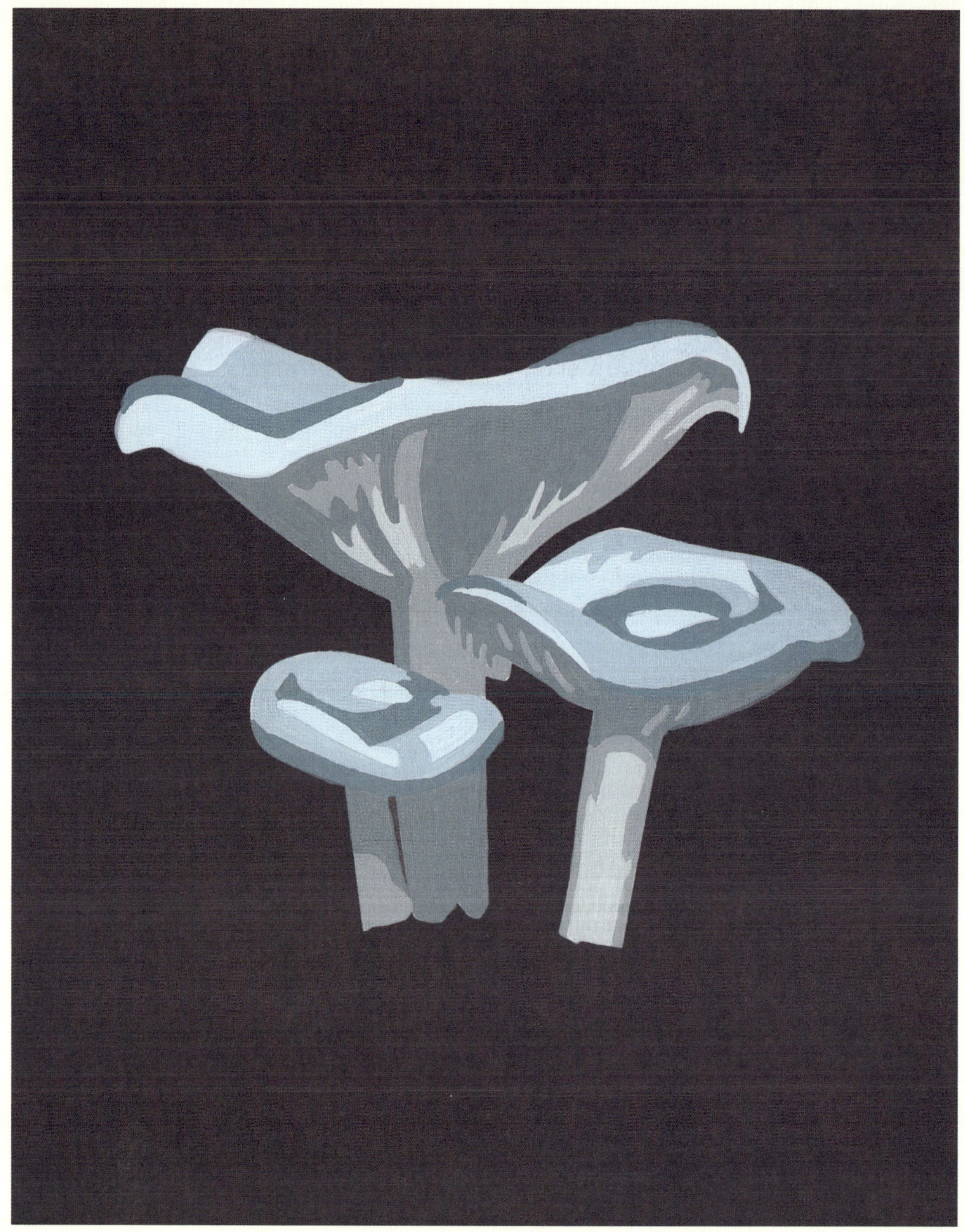

ANISEED TOADSTOOL

Clitocybe odora

ANISEED TOADSTOOL

CLITOCYBE ODORA

NATURE'S TERRIBLE TWIZZLER

If the name didn't give it away, you must know that this mushie smells (and tastes) like anise or lico-rice. It's edible when cooked but usually used in small doses like a spice instead of its full mushroom form. It can be confused for the toxic *Clitocybe fragrans* because they share a similar smell, but they look fairly different. *Odora* is more of a grayish blue-green, while *fragrans* is more of a creamy tan.

Maggots love these 'shrooms, too. So sometimes you'll find them infested with these creepy crawlers in the wild. They grow from summer to fall in the shadows of trees, among the leaf litter. You'll see them growing throughout the UK and in the US from the Midwest to the Northwest.

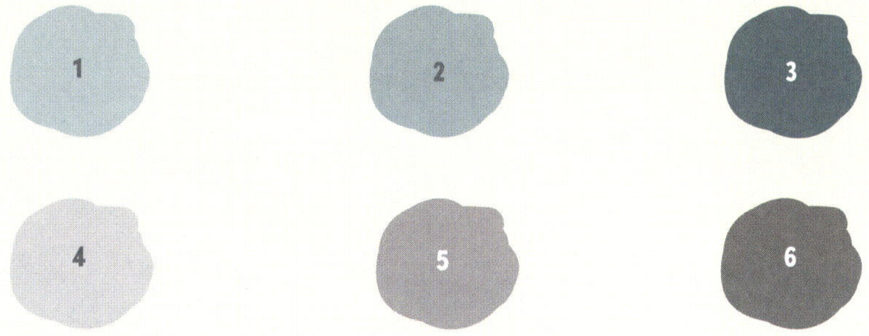

TO BLEND YOUR OWN COLORS FOR THIS PRINT, SEE PAGE 99 FOR
BLENDING RECIPES AND SWATCH SAMPLES.

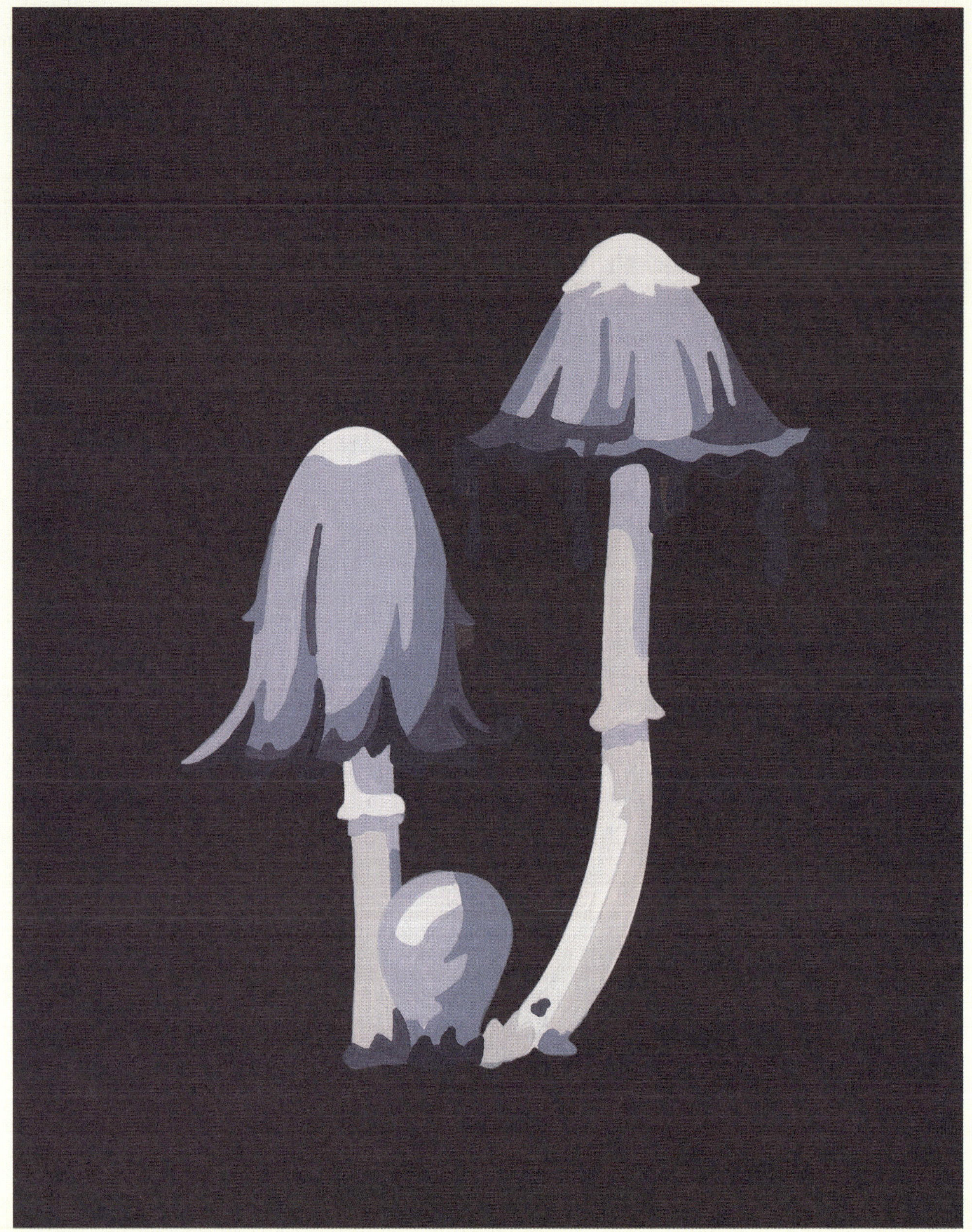

INKY CAP

Coprinopsis atramentaria

INKY CAP

COPRINOPSIS ATRAMENTARIA

MUSHROOM BEFORE LIQUOR, NEVER BEEN SICKER

This isn't called inky just because of its charcoal exterior. It used to be used to make ink, since a viscous liquid oozes from the gills of this toadstool as it ages. Sounds inedible, right? Actually, you can eat this mushroom as long as it's cooked and you don't consume any liquor before or after eating it. If you munch on this alongside your favorite cocktail, it can be poisonous.

They're a pretty common fungus, growing in both wild and city environments. They've even been known to break through asphalt as they grow, but you'll likely find them growing in clusters from tree stumps or wherever there's buried wood.

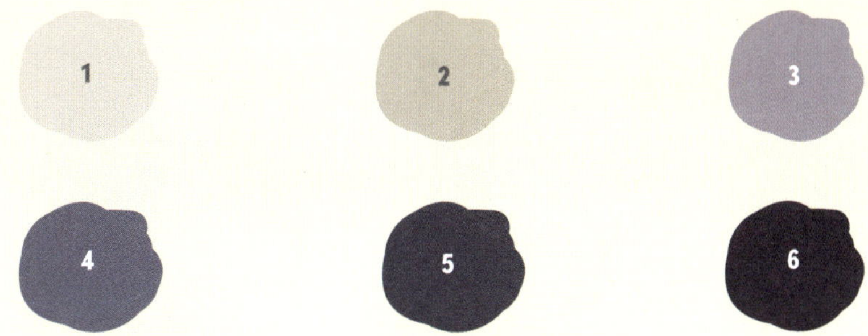

TO BLEND YOUR OWN COLORS FOR THIS PRINT, SEE PAGE 99 FOR
BLENDING RECIPES AND SWATCH SAMPLES.

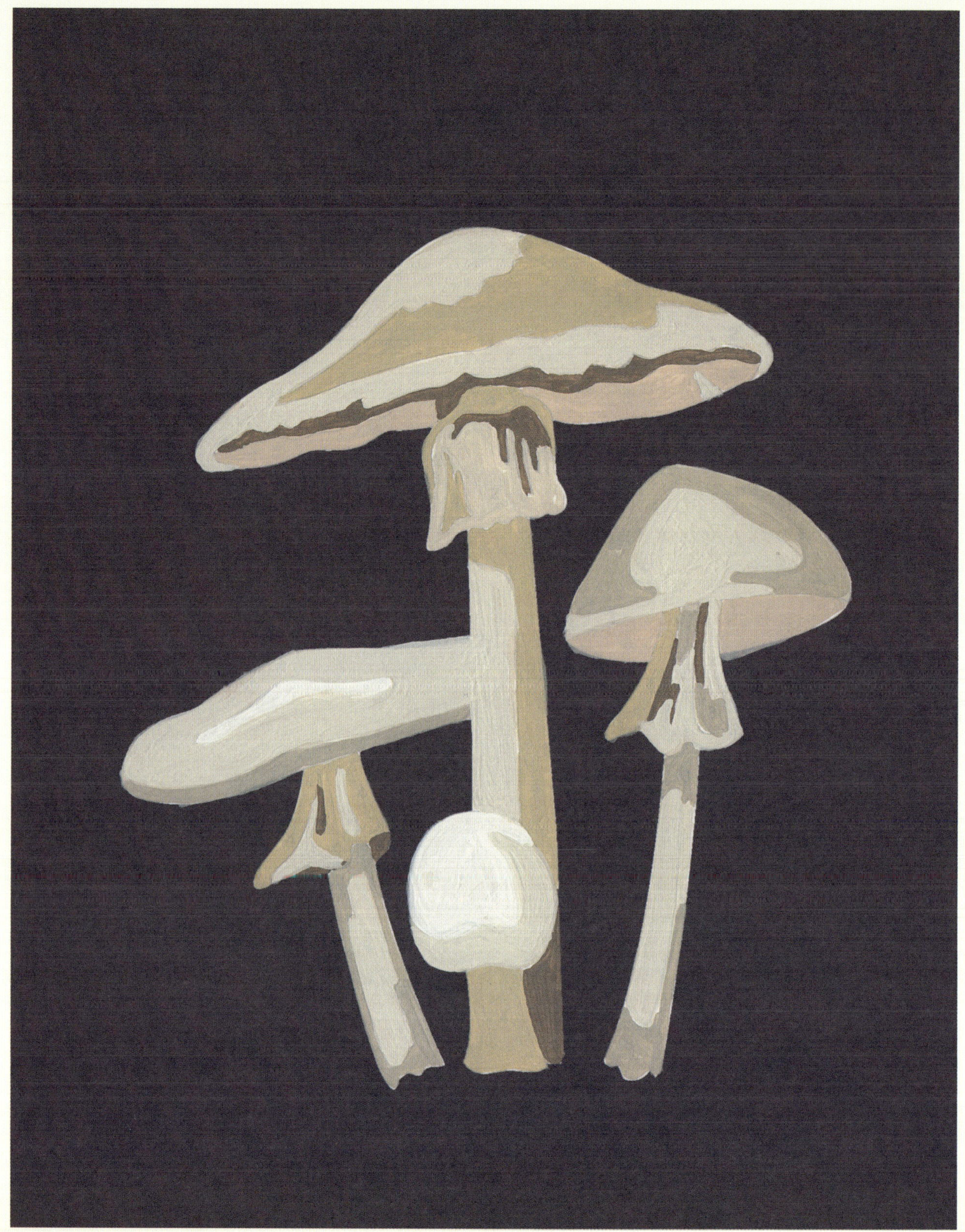

DESTROYING ANGEL

Amanita virosa

DESTROYING ANGEL

AMANITA VIROSA

THIS AIN'T NO ANGEL

Think of the destroying angel as a close cousin of the death cap (they're sometimes even called white death caps). They're both in the Amanita genus, and they're both highly poisonous. The tricky thing about the A. virosa is that it looks super similar to the edible white button mushroom, but one way you can tell the difference is by cutting it in half. Apparently, their internal structures look highly different, but you'll need to know what you're looking for to be sure.

And the A. virosa isn't the only species called a destroying angel. There are four that go by that common name, which are: Amanita bisporigera, Amanita ocreata, Amanita virosa, and Amanita verna. These toadstools can be found growing throughout North America, connected to tree roots in forests from the East Coast to the West Coast.

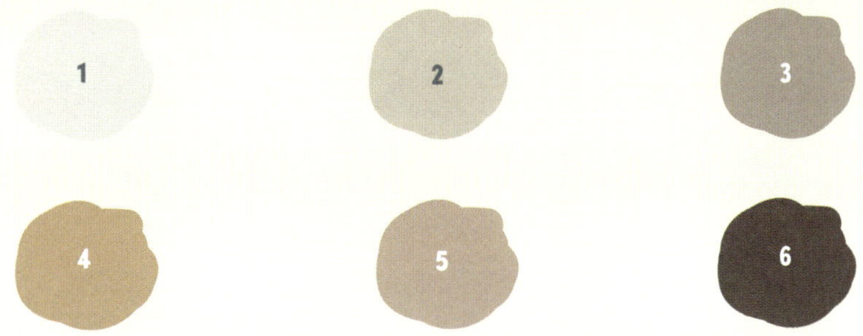

TO BLEND YOUR OWN COLORS FOR THIS PRINT, SEE PAGE 101 FOR BLENDING RECIPES AND SWATCH SAMPLES.

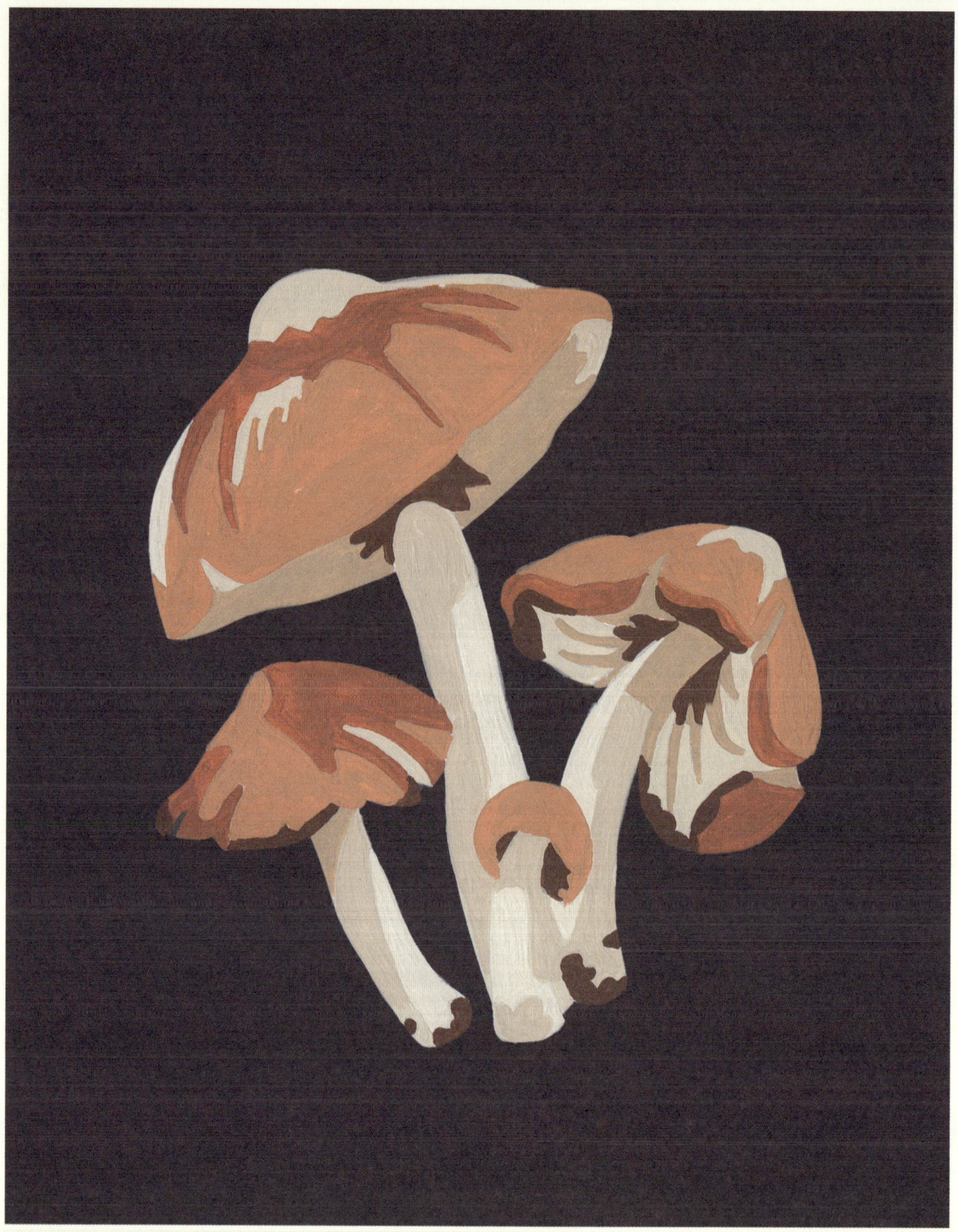

DEADLY FIBRECAP

Inocybe erubescens

DEADLY FIBRECAP

INOCYBE ERUBESCENS

IF IT BLEEDS, IT LEADS . . . TO DEATH

Most mushrooms in the genus *Inocybe* are toxic, and the red-staining variety is considered to be the most poisonous. It starts off a pale white and may look similar to the St. George's mushroom (*Calocybe gambosa*), which is edible when cooked. But the *gambosa* stays pale throughout, while this toadstool takes on an inky rust color once cut or bruised, or as it ages. Almost like seeping blood.

Like your ex, it has some surface good qualities: It smells great, similar to honey or perfumed soap, but once you dig deeper, it's all bad news. It can cause diarrhea, gastric upset, the sweats, and even death. It grows in open forests, usually in leaf litter of beech trees and in chalky soils.

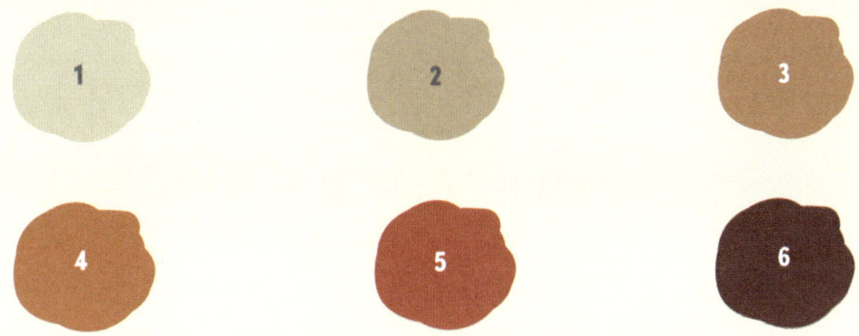

TO BLEND YOUR OWN COLORS FOR THIS PRINT, SEE PAGE 101 FOR BLENDING RECIPES AND SWATCH SAMPLES.

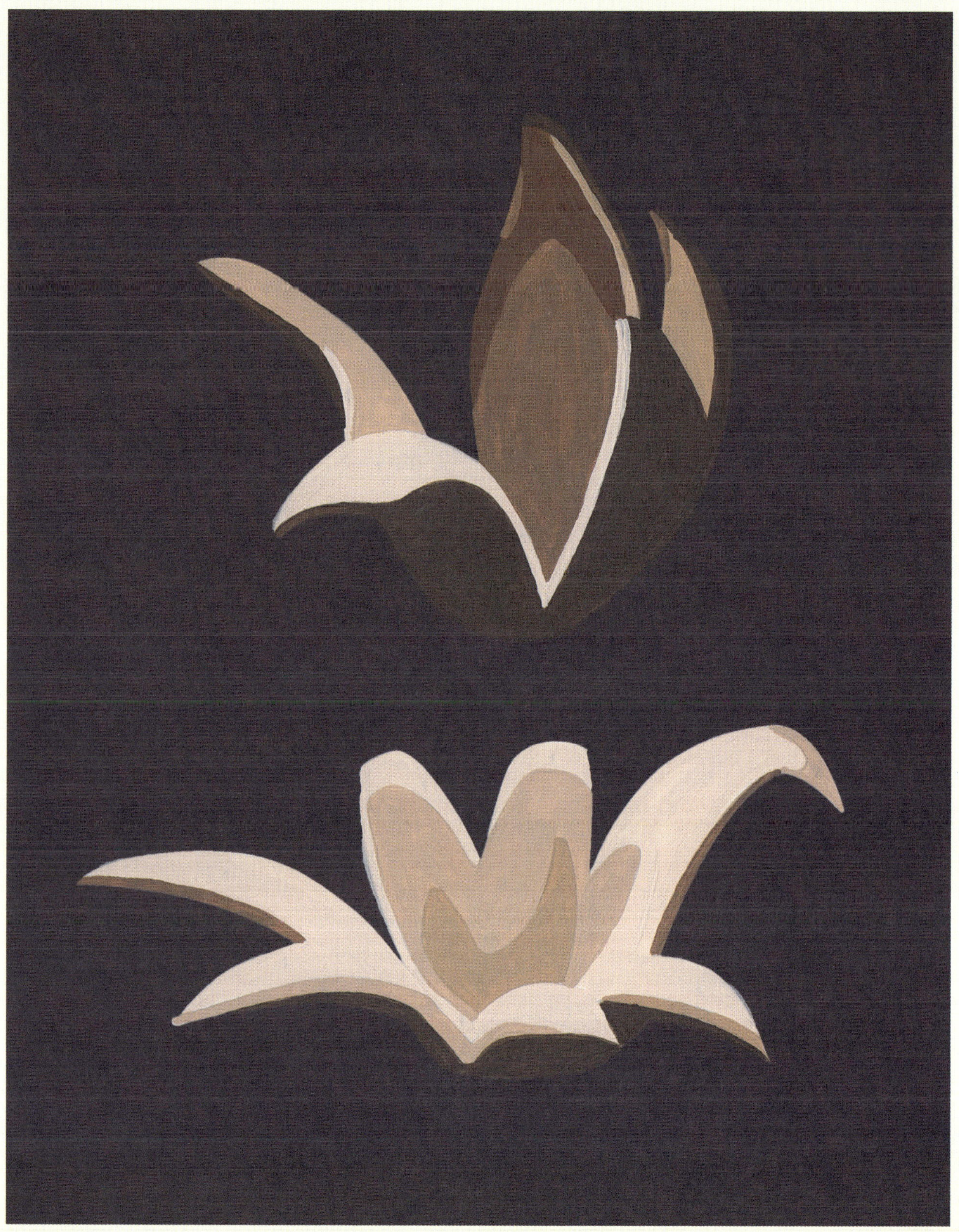

DEVIL'S CIGAR

Chorioactis geaster

DEVIL'S CIGAR

CHORIOACTIS GEASTER

DON'T MESS WITH TEXAS (MUSHROOMS)

This delight only grows in Texas and sometimes Japan. It's a beautiful flower-shaped mushroom that is pretty rare. So why's it called a devil's cigar? Before it "blooms" into its final state, it grows in a curled-up shape in clusters that look very similar to a bunch of discarded unsmoked cigars. Apparently, when it unfurls, the fungus actually hisses at you. It also goes by the name Texas star and is the official fungus of the Lone Star State.

If you want to find this brown, fuzzy star in the wild, search around central and north Texas in late fall. You'll find it growing on dead cedar elm stumps or roots. Don't eat it, though. It's not poisonous, but it isn't edible.

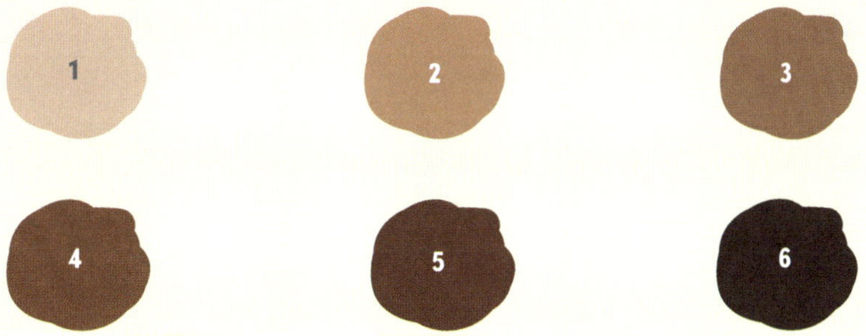

TO BLEND YOUR OWN COLORS FOR THIS PRINT, SEE PAGE 101 FOR
BLENDING RECIPES AND SWATCH SAMPLES.

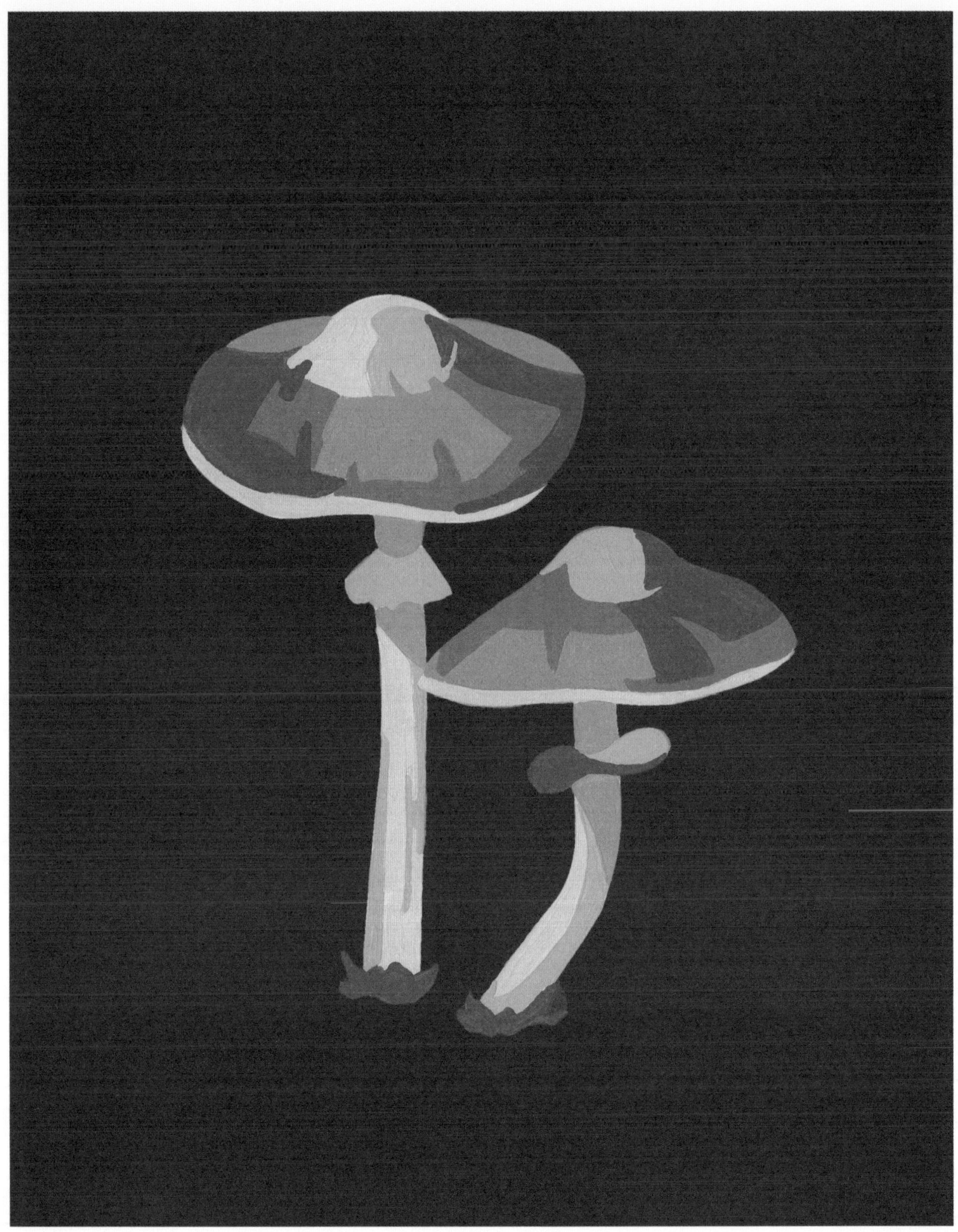

VERDIGRIS AGARIC

Stropharia aeruginosa

VERDIGRIS AGARIC

STROPHARIA AERUGINOSA

CAN MUSHROOMS BE PRETTY?

This one certainly is. The first thing that might stand out to you when coming across this 'shroom: the beautiful aqua-green color. It's downright gorgeous. The name verdigris actually comes from the old French vert d'*aigre*, meaning "green [made by action] of vinegar," which is what happens when copper patinas. Know what else shares this blue-green color? The Statue of Liberty.

But this fungus is about more than its looks. It also supposedly has toxic levels of the hallucinogen psilocybin. So you don't want to eat this (unless you want to travel to the stratosphere . . . or spend all day in the bathroom). If you're trying to find it in the wild, try searching around Britain and Ireland from July to October. It's usually found in grassy woods, growing on rotten logs, or within mulchy areas. But be aware that its pretty color doesn't last long. As the mushroom ages, it loses its hue and will look closer to a pale tan, gray, or even white.

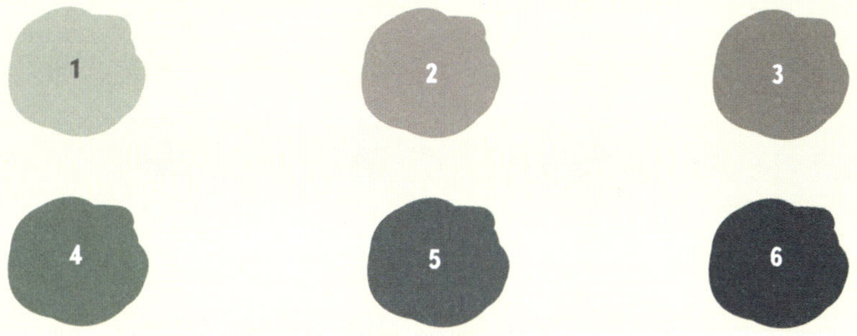

TO BLEND YOUR OWN COLORS FOR THIS PRINT, SEE PAGE 103 FOR
BLENDING RECIPES AND SWATCH SAMPLES.

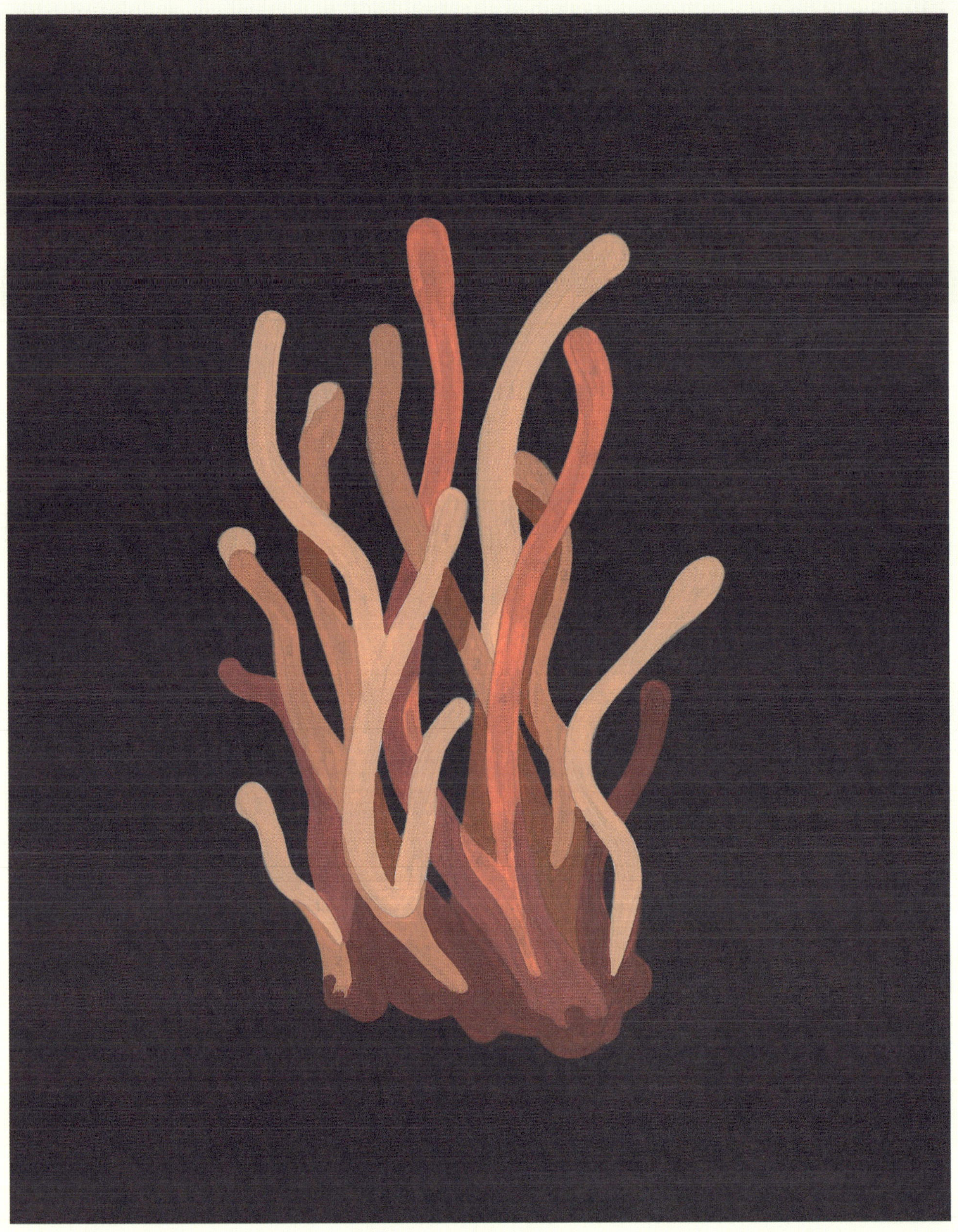

SCARLET CATERPILLAR CLUB

Cordyceps militaris

SCARLET CATERPILLAR CLUB

CORDYCEPS MILITARIS

FINALLY, A CLUB WITH A LOW BARRIER OF ENTRY

If you're wondering why the term *cordyceps* sounds familiar, it's because that's the genus of 'shrooms fictionalized on the show *The Last of Us* that turns humans into mindless zombies. But this fungus is only harmful to moth or butterfly larvae, which it infiltrates and infects for its own growth and survival.

For humans, these fingerlike fungi have been used in traditional Chinese medicine, and may even be found as a vitamin supplement in China. They can be cultivated in a lab and supposedly have anti-inflammatory properties, as well as purported benefits for your liver, kidneys, and sex drive.

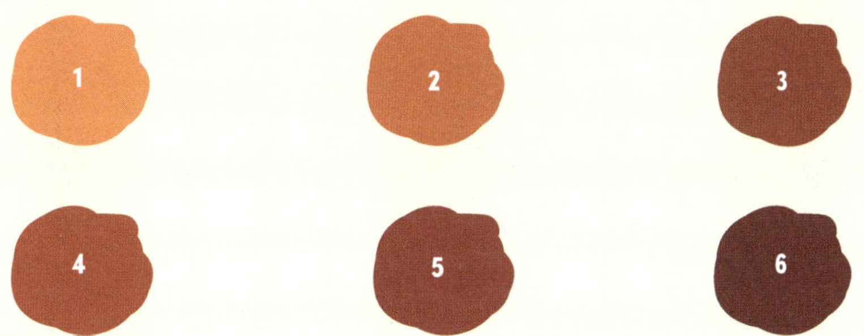

TO BLEND YOUR OWN COLORS FOR THIS PRINT, SEE PAGE 103 FOR BLENDING RECIPES AND SWATCH SAMPLES.

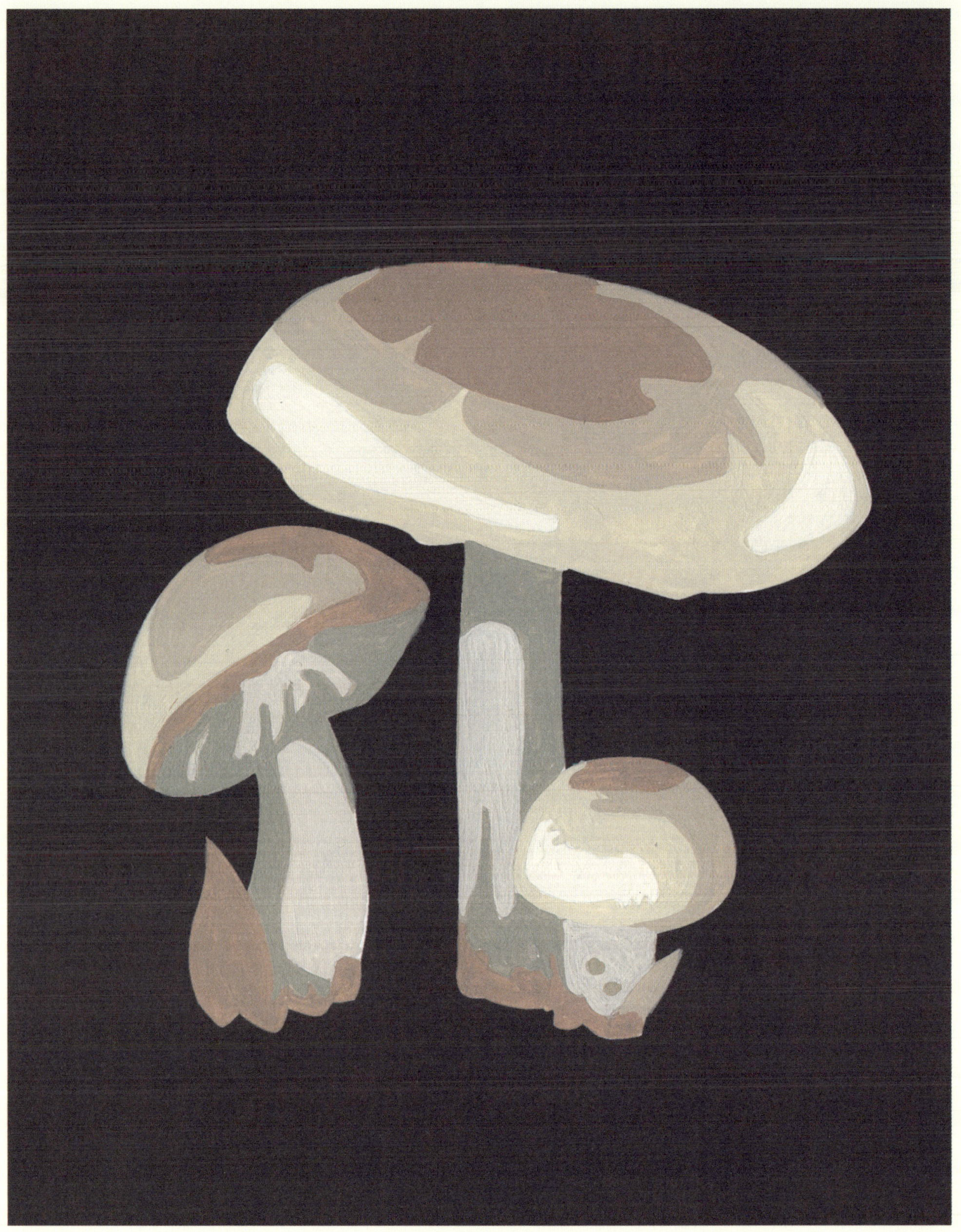

DEATH CAP

Amanita phalloides

DEATH CAP

AMANITA PHALLOIDES

MORE TOXIC THAN YOUR EX

Just in case the name wasn't a giveaway: *This will kill you.* This is considered the GOAT of all toxic fungi and is likely responsible for the majority of mushroom poisonings around the world. Where can you find them? Oh, mostly everywhere except Antarctica. On the East Coast, they like to grow near pines, and on the West Coast, they like to grow near oak trees. Some may even grow in your own backyard.

The way it kills is deceptive. Eight to 12 hours after eating them, you'll get some gnarly symptoms like vomiting and a crampy stomach, but by the time you hit the 24-hour mark, you'll probably feel better. The main show starts around 72 hours after that first bite, with symptoms like liver or kidney failure, seizures, or coma. Milk thistle might be an antidote, but that isn't proven. Usually, treatment includes aggressive hydration and may require some kind of organ transplant (likely liver), depending on the severity of symptoms.

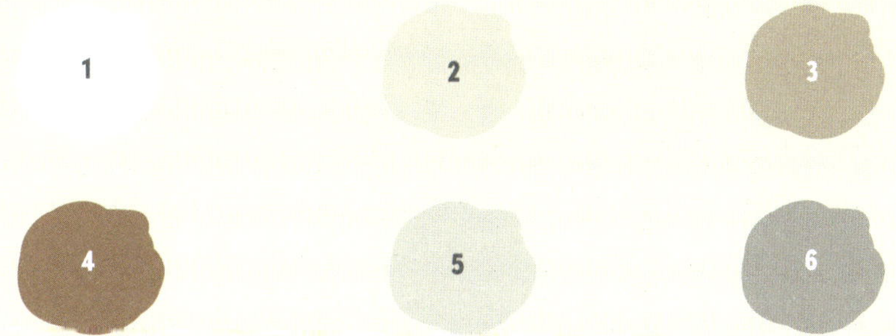

TO BLEND YOUR OWN COLORS FOR THIS PRINT, SEE PAGE 103 FOR
BLENDING RECIPES AND SWATCH SAMPLES.

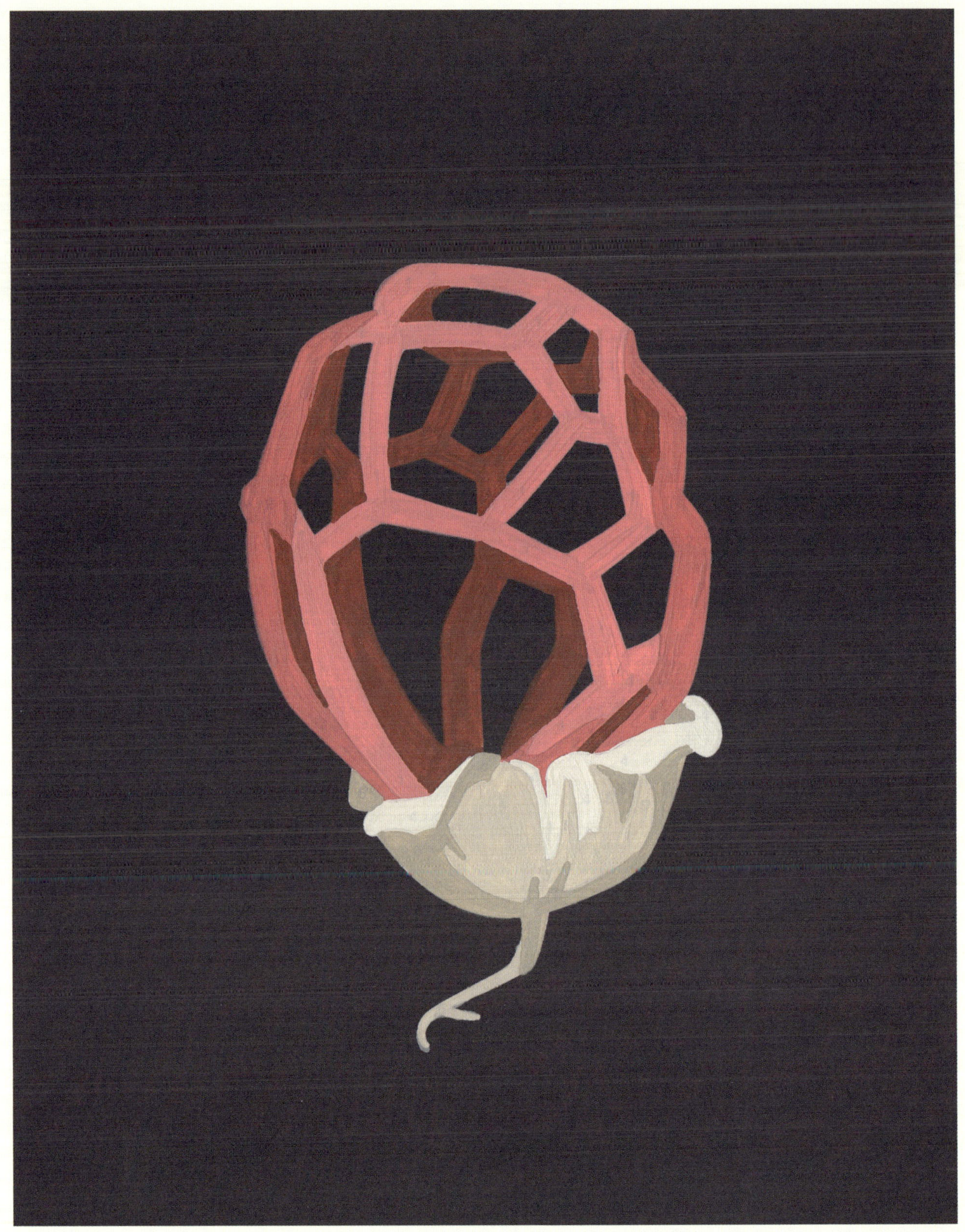

LATTICED STINKHORN

Clathrus ruber

LATTICED STINKHORN

CLATHRUS RUBER

SOMETIMES YOU'VE GOTTA STOP AND SMELL THE ROTTEN STEAK

This isn't your average-looking mushie. And if you have trypophobia (an aversion to the sight of irregular patterns or clusters of small holes or bumps), you might want to stay away. Its cap is less mushroom and more Wiffle ball, with a geometric resemblance to lace. It can be orangey-red or red-red, and I wouldn't be surprised if someone told us it had an alien origin. The fungus grows from spores that look like tiny white eggs.

The most distinctive thing about this mushroom, though? It has a rancid smell—like a cross between rotting steak and a decaying dead rat under your dishwasher. Apparently, this perfume attracts flies, which helps this mushroom distribute its spores and reproduce. Want to hear the wild part? It's edible in its immature stage when cooked. And in some places, it's even considered a delicacy. Pass the stinkhorn, please.

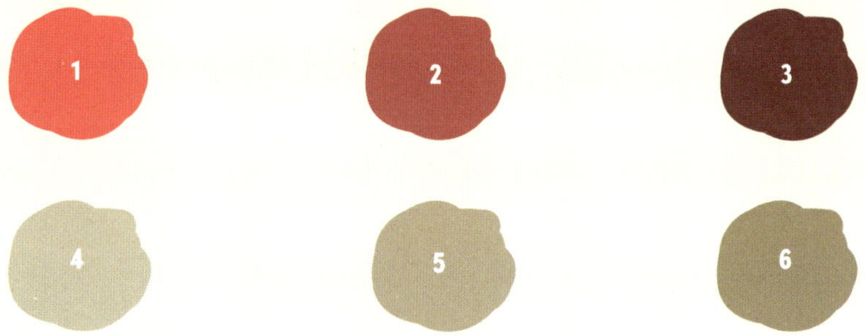

TO BLEND YOUR OWN COLORS FOR THIS PRINT, SEE PAGE 105 FOR BLENDING RECIPES AND SWATCH SAMPLES.

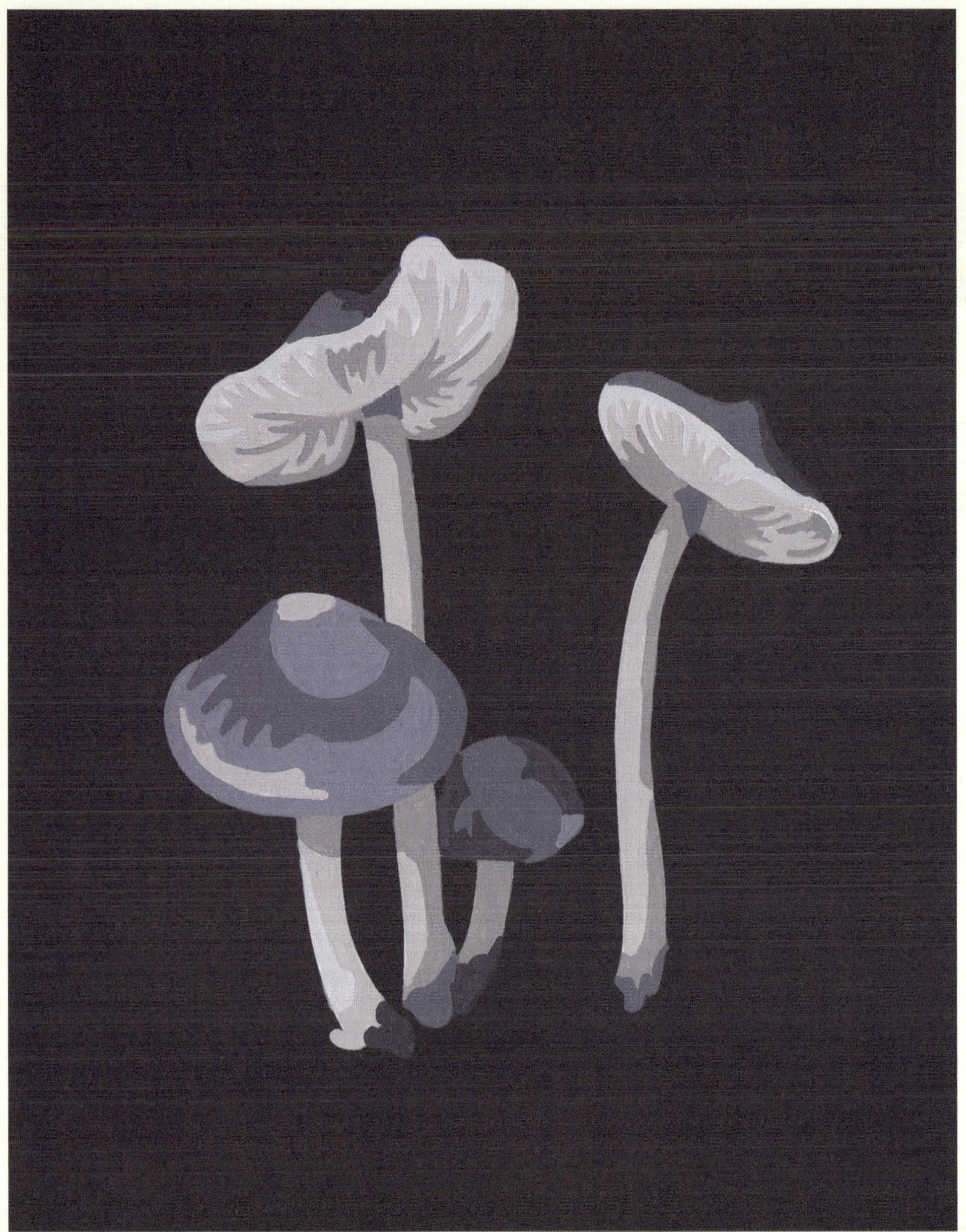

LILAC BONNET

Mycena pura

LILAC BONNET

MYCENA PURA

ALL THE BEAUTY OF A MONDAY MORNING IN ONE LITTLE MUSHROOM

This petite lavender toadstool is deceptive. While it may look innocent, it actually contains muscarine, the same chemical that makes the fly agaric poisonous. If you mistake its radishlike smell (and taste) for edibility, you'll likely find yourself with decreased blood pressure, excessive sweating, exhaustion, and irritability and, well, feeling like me on a Monday morning.

In some cases, it can cause more severe symptoms and could even be fatal. It's sometimes called a poison radish. The purple coloring isn't a reliable way to know if the 'shroom you've found is actually a *Mycena pura*. Their caps can also be blue, light yellow, or white. And if it's pink, you might have found a rosy bonnet. These two species are sometimes mistaken for each other, but rosy is often larger and pinker.

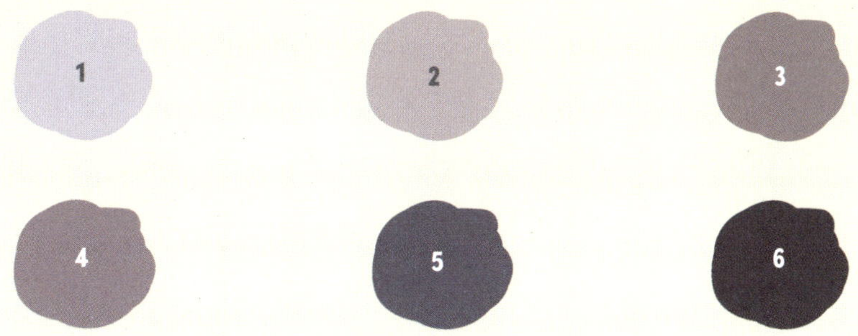

TO BLEND YOUR OWN COLORS FOR THIS PRINT, SEE PAGE 105 FOR BLENDING RECIPES AND SWATCH SAMPLES.

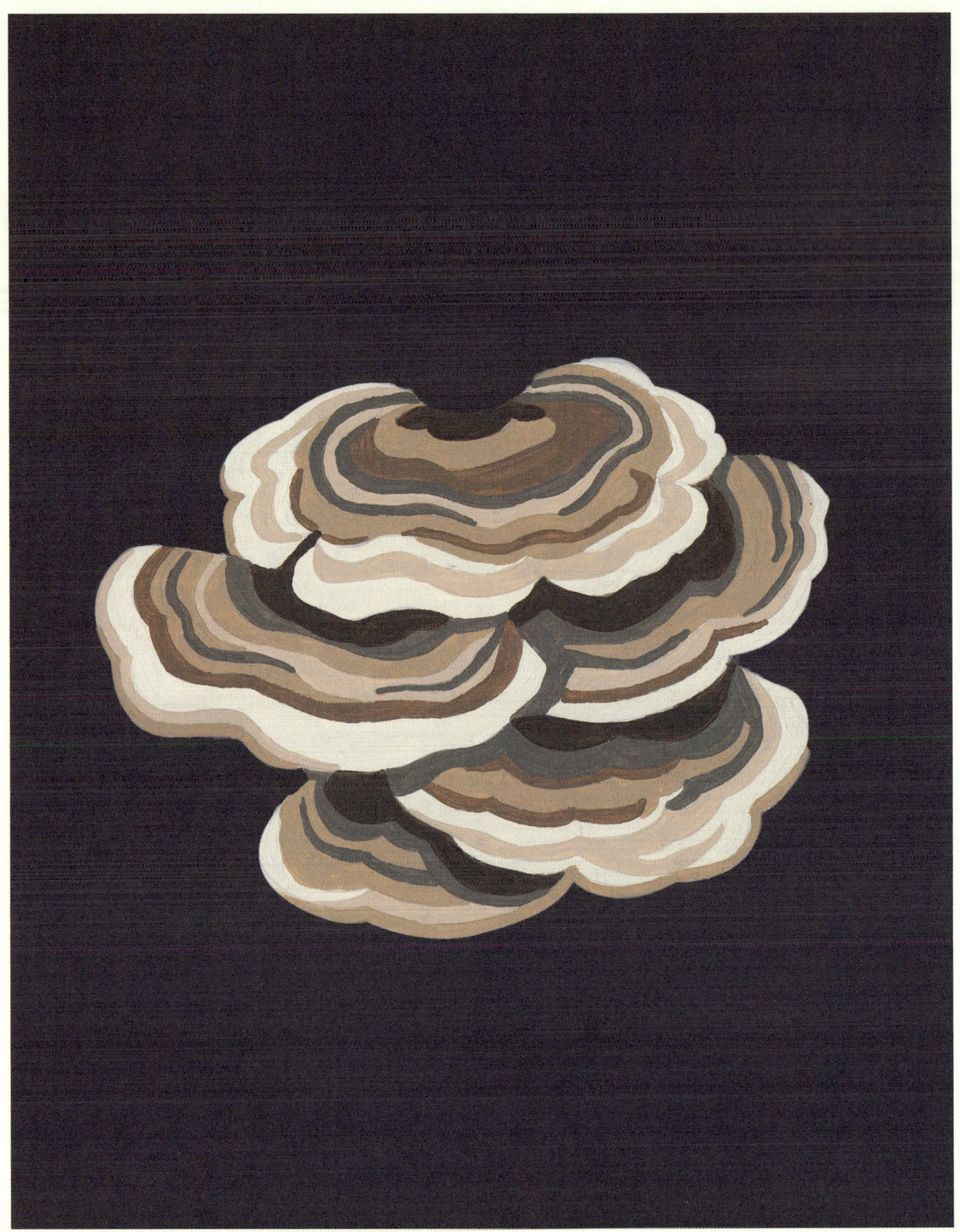

TURKEY TAIL

Trametes versicolor

TURKEY TAIL

TRAMETES VERSICOLOR

HE'S A LOVER, NOT A FIGHTER

Some mushrooms are all about killing, but this one is all about healing. This funky-looking 'shroom is known for its supposed medicinal properties and can be found growing on stumps and logs. It doesn't look like your typical toadstool, since it doesn't have a stalk nor does it grow with that signature cap.

The turkey tail is purported to have antioxidants that can help boost your immune system and prebiotics that can help with your gut health. But the most interesting and amazing claim is that this fungus might have the ability to help fight cancer and prevent tumors. More scientific studies are needed to prove these claims, but the turkey tail has been used in Chinese and Japanese medicine. They're usually consumed in tea form, as a powder, or as pills.

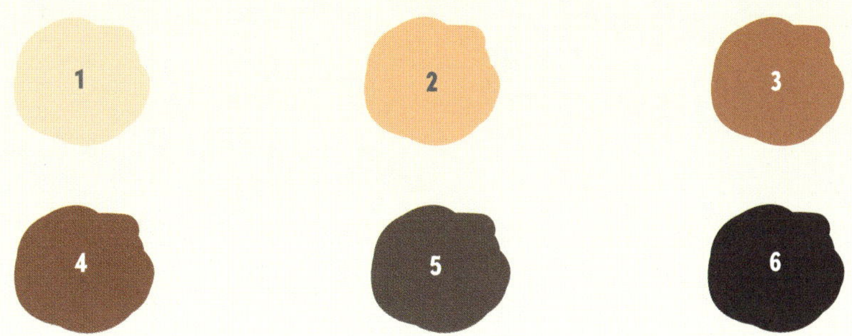

TO BLEND YOUR OWN COLORS FOR THIS PRINT, SEE PAGE 105 FOR BLENDING RECIPES AND SWATCH SAMPLES.

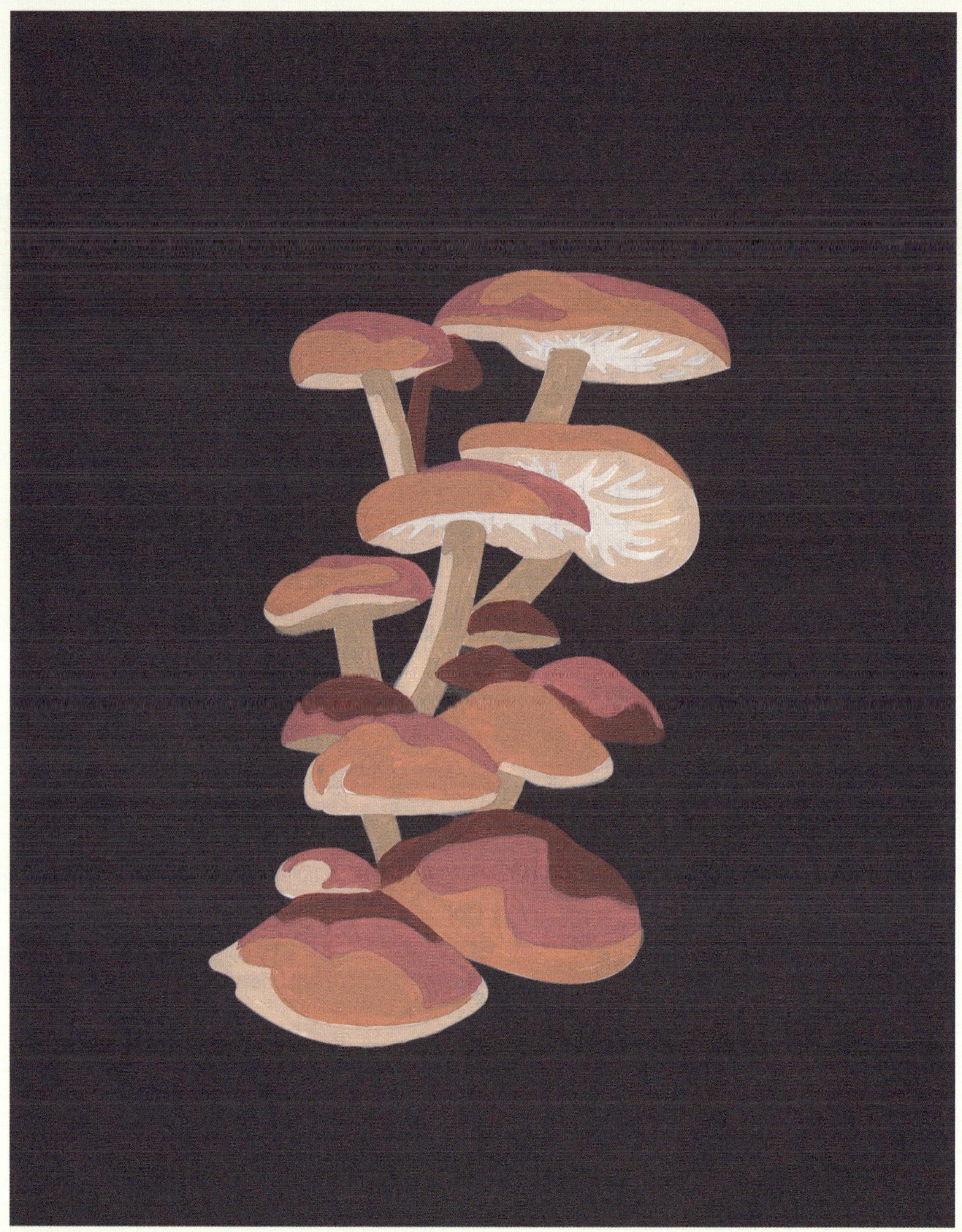

VELVET SHANK

Flammulina velutipes

VELVET SHANK

FLAMMULINA VELUTIPES

FRIENDLIER THAN YOUR AVERAGE JAILHOUSE SHANK

You might have eaten these and never even realized it. The cultivated version of this fungus can be found in most grocery stores and is known as enoki mushroom (or enokitake). But they look completely different in their tame state. They're smaller-capped, white, and have thin, long stems. I prefer the wild version, with its burnt orangey brown caps and velvety stems.

These mushrooms are purported to have some anticancer properties, but more research would be needed to know for sure. One last thing: This version is edible when cooked, but there's another type of mushroom, *Galerina autumnalis* (a.k.a. deadly skullcap), that looks almost identical to the velvet shank but most definitely is not. So make sure you know which one you're planning to eat if you don't want to get shanked.

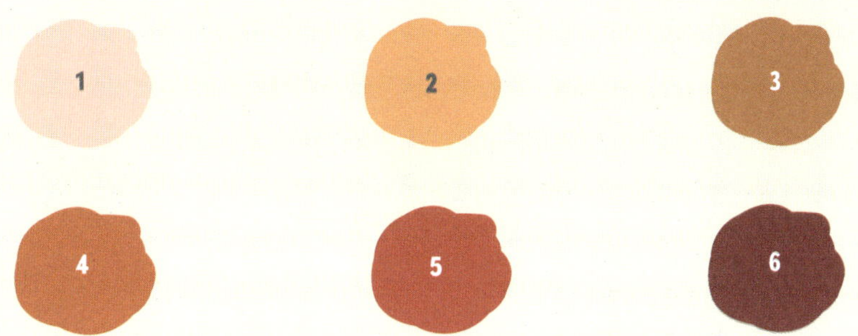

TO BLEND YOUR OWN COLORS FOR THIS PRINT, SEE PAGE 107 FOR BLENDING RECIPES AND SWATCH SAMPLES.

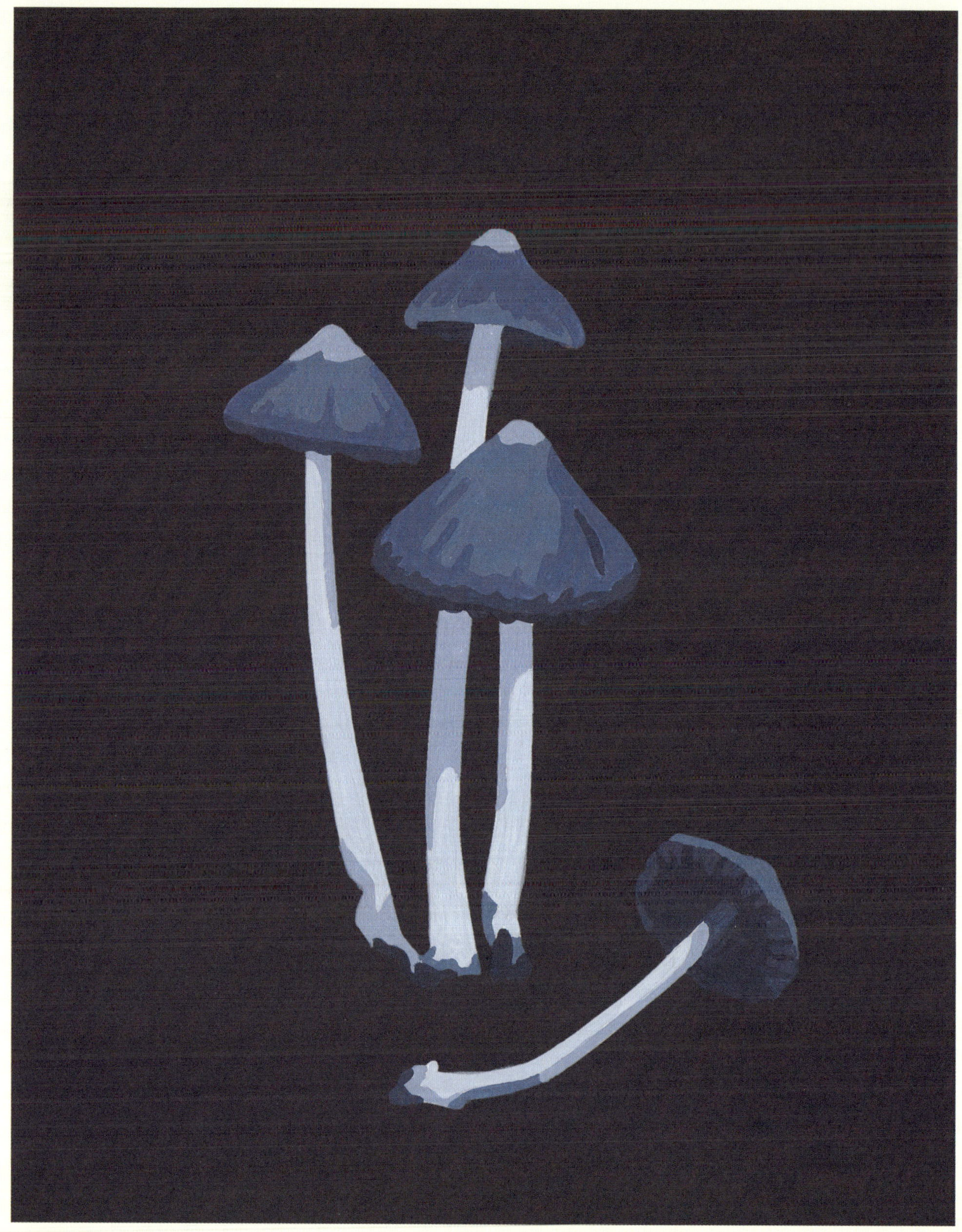

SKY-BLUE MUSHROOM

Entoloma hochstetteri

SKY-BLUE MUSHROOM

ENTOLOMA HOCHSTETTERI

BRIGHT BLUE DYE FOR BABY BIRD BEAKS

The first thing you'll notice is the brilliant sapphire color of this toadstool. It almost looks fake because of how saturated it is with color. Native to New Zealand, you'll find it on their $50 bill next to the extinct kōkako bird, whose wattle is also bright blue. Māori lore says the bird got its blue coloring by rubbing up against this mushroom, and the two have been intertwined ever since.

The color looks trippy, but it won't actually send you on a trip. It doesn't contain psilocybin or any other mind-bending properties, but it also isn't edible. Just think of it as eye candy. One last fact about sky-blue? The blue doesn't go all the way through. Its gills and spore prints are a lovely shade of blush.

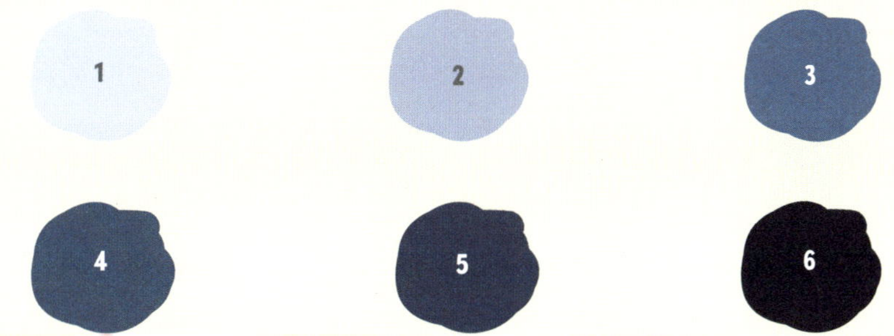

TO BLEND YOUR OWN COLORS FOR THIS PRINT, SEE PAGE 107 FOR BLENDING RECIPES AND SWATCH SAMPLES.

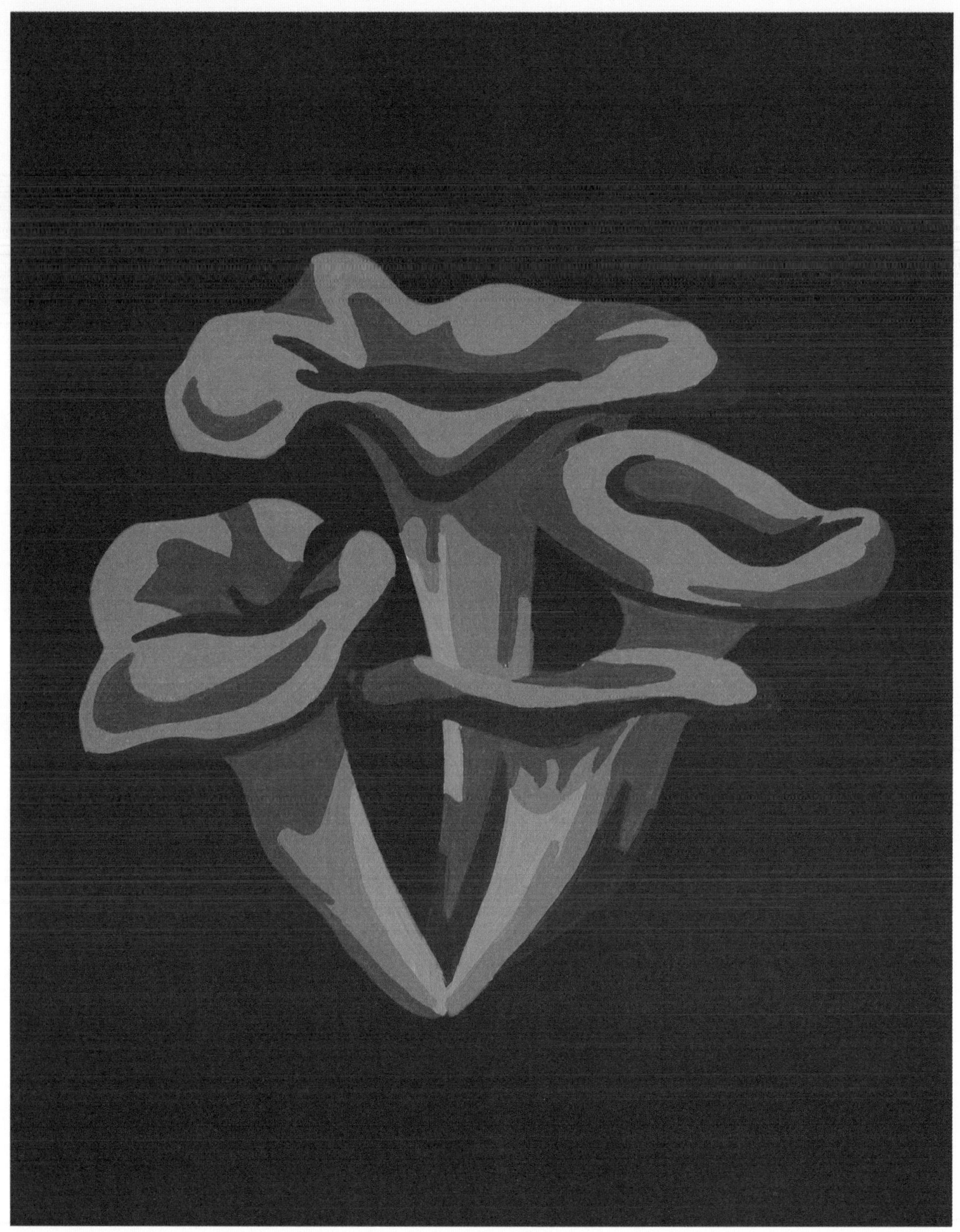

BLACK TRUMPET

Craterellus cornucopioides

BLACK TRUMPET

CRATERELLUS CORNUCOPIOIDES

NOW YOU'VE GOT A STEW GOIN'

If a mushroom's other name is trumpet of death or devil's horn, and it has an inky dark color that seems like the color of poison, would you think it was edible? And not just edible but really delicious? Well, quit judgin', Mr. McJudgey, because this mushie is 100 percent edible when cooked and even considered gourmet.

They taste similar to the more expensive truffle mushroom, with a nice mix of smoky and fruity, a deep umami flavor. The flavor is enhanced when dried, so some people dehydrate them and turn them into a powder before they add them to soups, stews, eggs, grits, vegetables, and more. They smell sort of like chanterelle mushrooms (kinda fruity, kinda floral) and can be found growing near the bottom of hardwood trees in late summer to early fall.

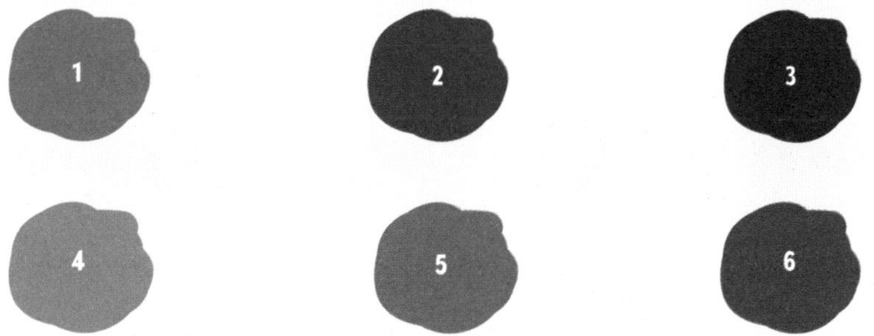

TO BLEND YOUR OWN COLORS FOR THIS PRINT, SEE PAGE 107 FOR BLENDING RECIPES AND SWATCH SAMPLES.

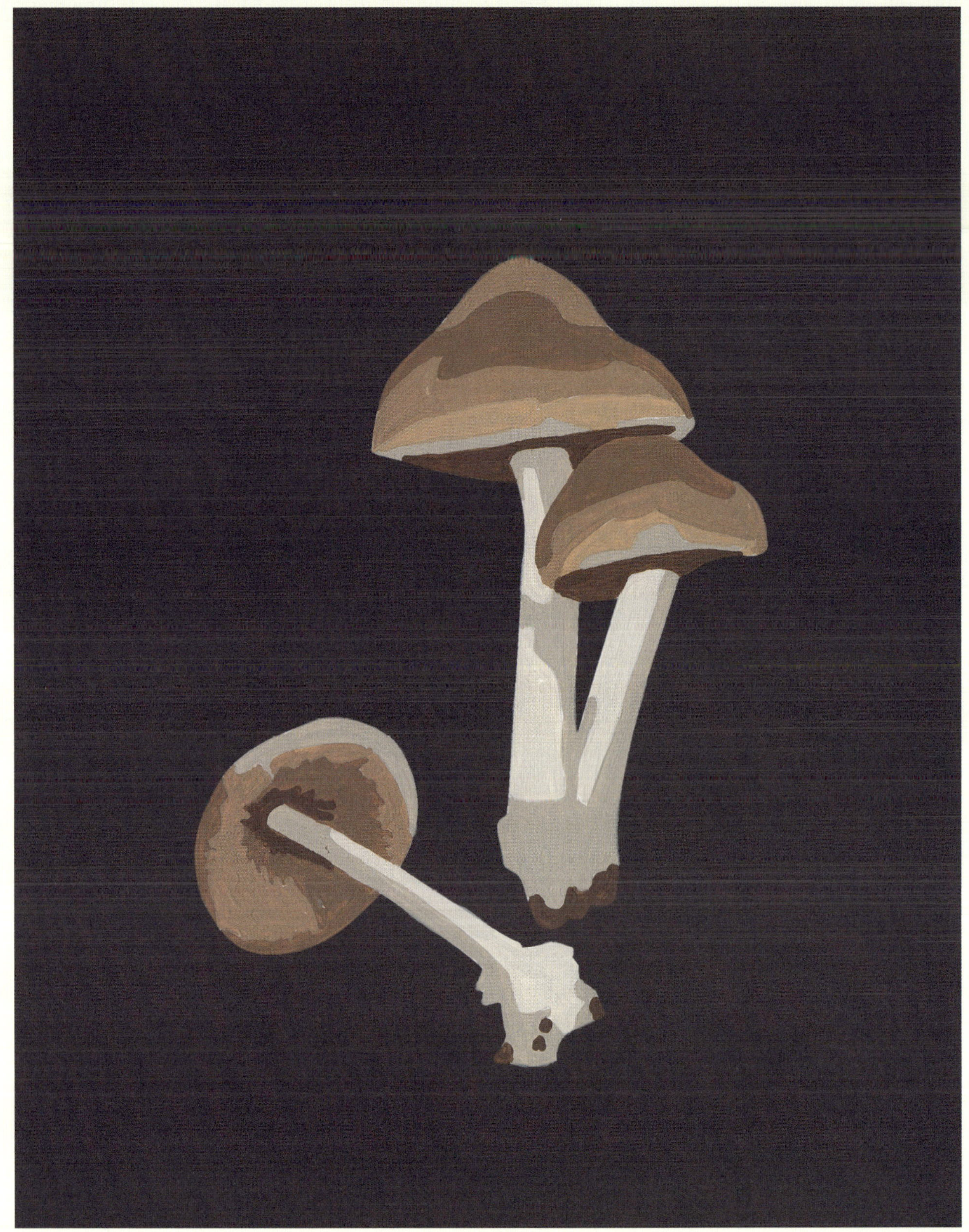

FLYING SAUCER

Psilocybe azurescens

FLYING SAUCER

PSILOCYBE AZURESCENS

THE MOST MAGICAL OF ALL MIND-BENDING MUSHIES

When *psilocybe* is in the name, you know you're about to go on a trip. In the book *How to Change Your Mind* (side note: highly recommend), author Michael Pollan forages for these 'shrooms under the pine trees across from the local police station. They're likely called flying saucers due to their shape and color, but others have said they're named for their ability to bring your mind straight to the cosmos.

While your brain might be vibing with these fun guys, your body might not. They're known to cause temporary paralysis. They grow all along the West Coast, from Oregon to California, mostly in sandy soil, beachy grasses, and wood chips.

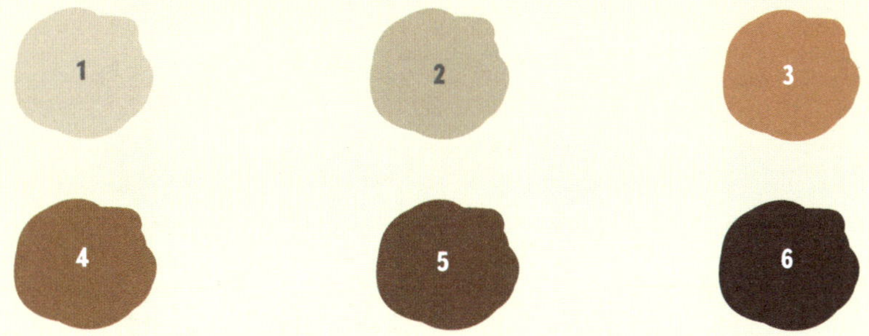

TO BLEND YOUR OWN COLORS FOR THIS PRINT, SEE PAGE 109 FOR
BLENDING RECIPES AND SWATCH SAMPLES.

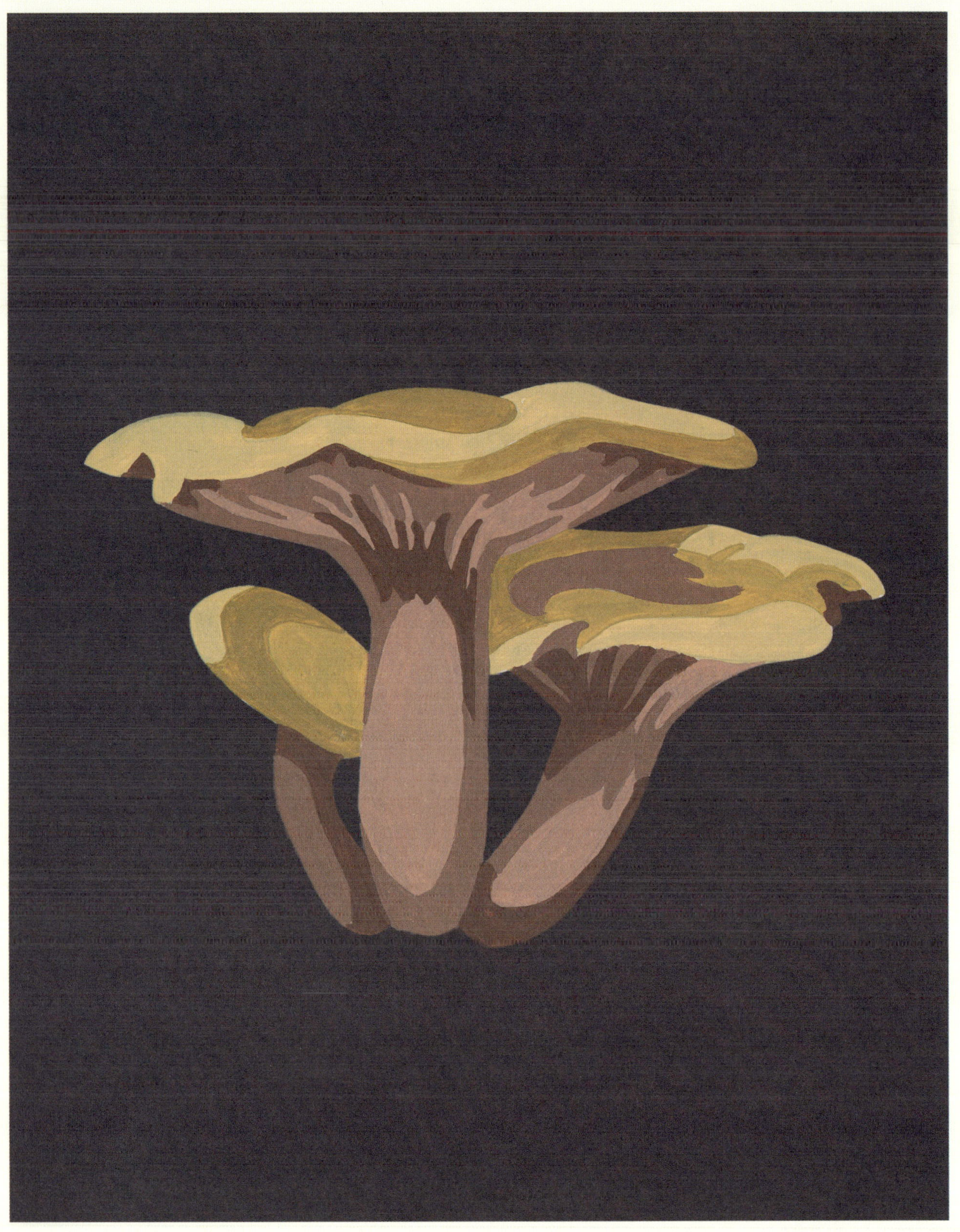

JACK-O'-LANTERN MUSHROOM

Omphalotus olearius

JACK-O'-LANTERN MUSHROOM

OMPHALOTUS OLEARIUS

HE'S POSITIVELY GLOWING

This burnt orange toadstool does a lot to live up to its name, with its pumpkinlike flesh on the outside and eerily glowy "insides." The glow actually comes from the gills and is most prominent on the younger mushrooms. If you take them to a dark place, you can see a blue-green bioluminescence shining through.

To an amateur mycologist, or someone who studies fungi, these might look like delicious chanterelles, but there are some distinct differences. They're poisonous for one. Another—when you peel the stem, you'll find them orange on the inside, while chanterelles are pale white inside. These grow mostly at the base of trees and stumps, in groups. They're found throughout Europe.

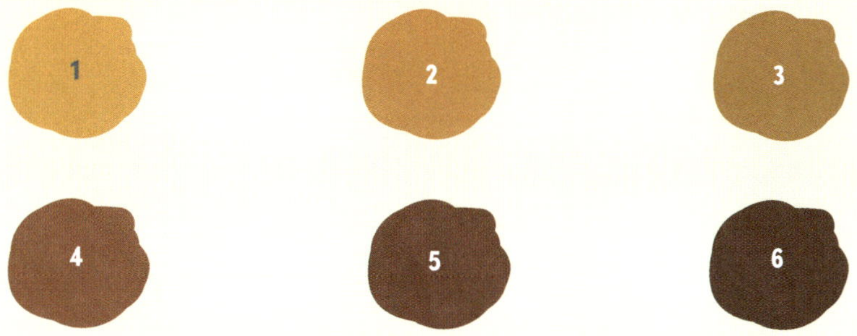

TO BLEND YOUR OWN COLORS FOR THIS PRINT, SEE PAGE 109 FOR
BLENDING RECIPES AND SWATCH SAMPLES.

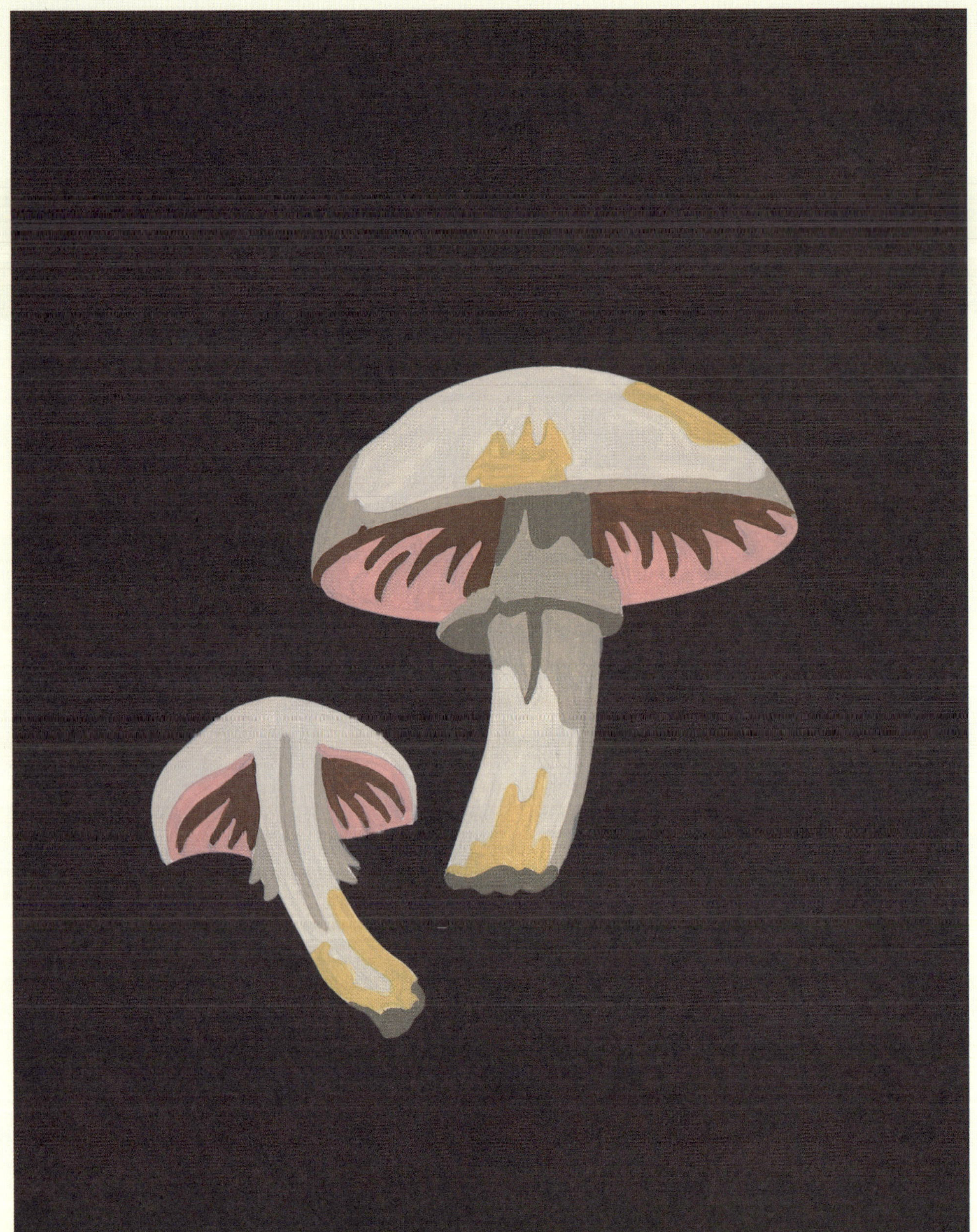

YELLOW STAINER

Agaricus xanthodermus

YELLOW STAINER

AGARICUS XANTHODERMUS

SOMETIMES YOU FEEL LIKE YOU'RE POISONED, SOMETIMES YOU DON'T

This toadstool is a real puzzle: It is mostly toxic to most people, but sometimes on others it has no effect at all. It starts off looking like any regular ol' white mushroom—in fact, it's suspiciously similar to the edible horse mushroom or field mushroom—but bruises yellow when pressed or cut. Oh, and this poisonous variety stinks when you cook it. It has an inky, woody, medicinal licorice smell. Hmmm, pass. I'm good.

It's a pretty common 'shroom that can be found in lawns, gardens, and woods, especially in California. And if you did consider yourself a gambler and tried to eat this mushroom, it probably wouldn't kill you, but it would give you a few gnarly days of symptoms that include stomach cramps, diarrhea, vomiting, and nausea. No, thanks.

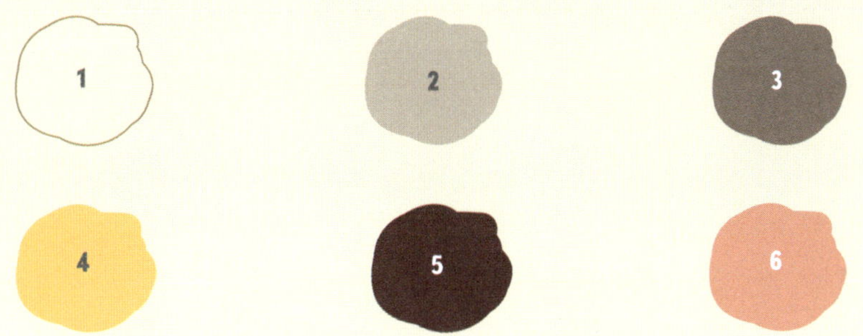

TO BLEND YOUR OWN COLORS FOR THIS PRINT, SEE PAGE 109 FOR BLENDING RECIPES AND SWATCH SAMPLES.

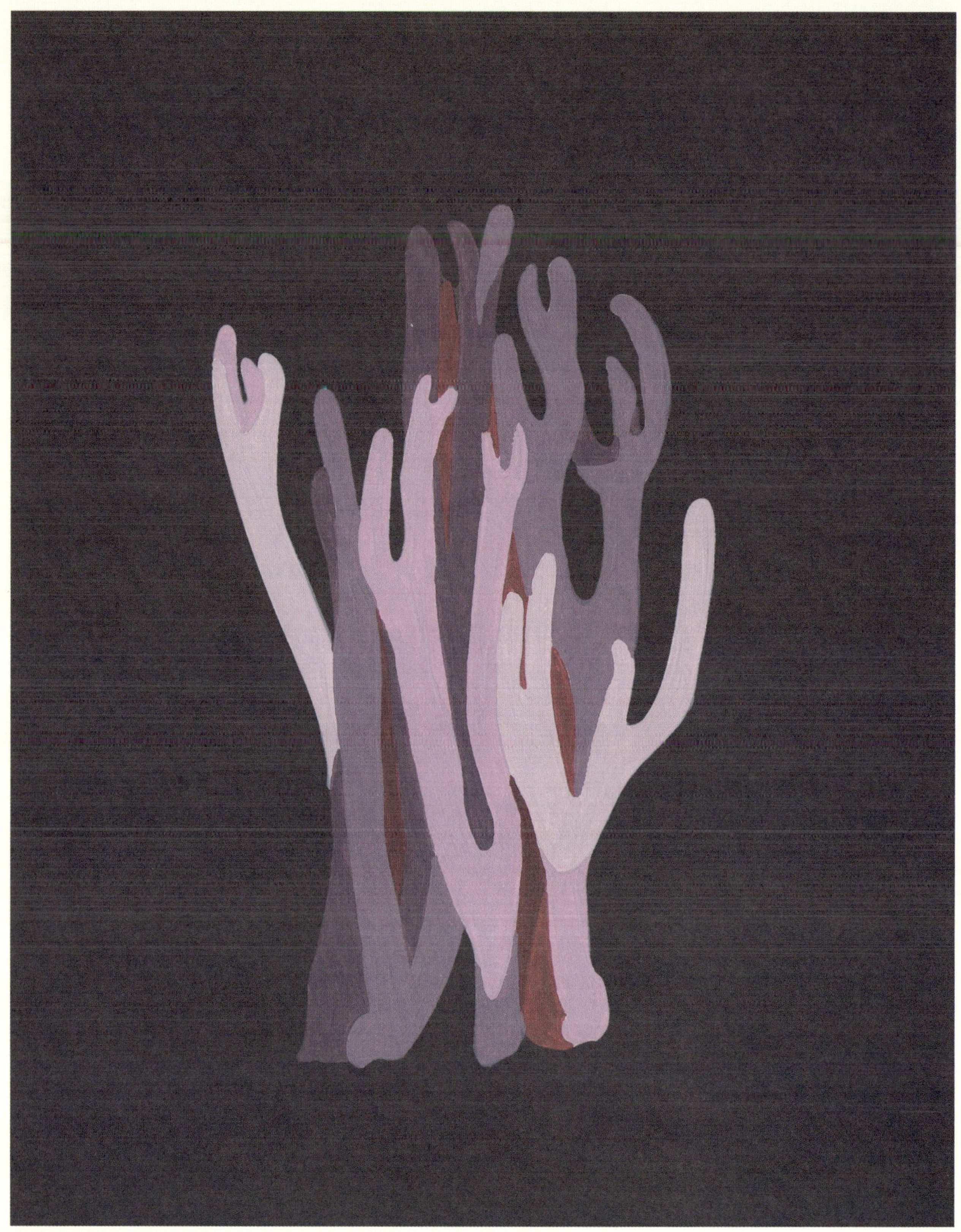

VIOLET CORAL

Clavaria zollingeri

VIOLET CORAL

CLAVARIA ZOLLINGERI

BEWARE OF THE PURPLE PEOPLE POOPER

Deep sea divers might recognize the beautiful antlerlike shape of these mushrooms as something they've come across underwater. The unique shape pairs nicely with the striking color—a bright pinkish-lavender that looks more like the product of food coloring than something you would find in the wild. These mushies are pretty rare because they like to grow in unfertilized grasslands.

Can you eat them? Well, technically yes if you've cooked them, and they taste kind of radishlike, but you might not want to unless you want to spend a whole day in the bathroom. These mushrooms are known to have a laxative effect when eaten, and some guides even label them inedible.

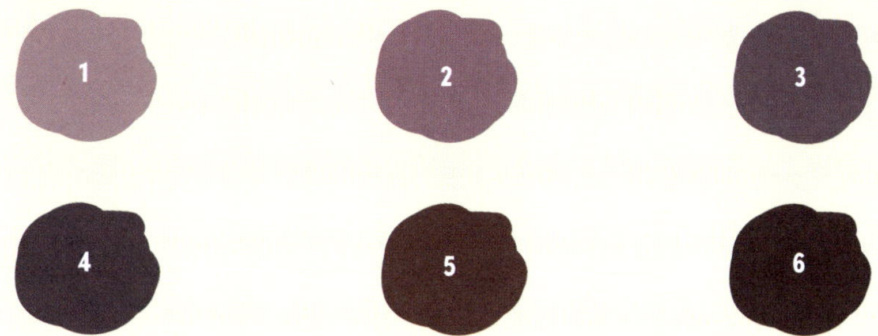

TO BLEND YOUR OWN COLORS FOR THIS PRINT, SEE PAGE 111 FOR
BLENDING RECIPES AND SWATCH SAMPLES.

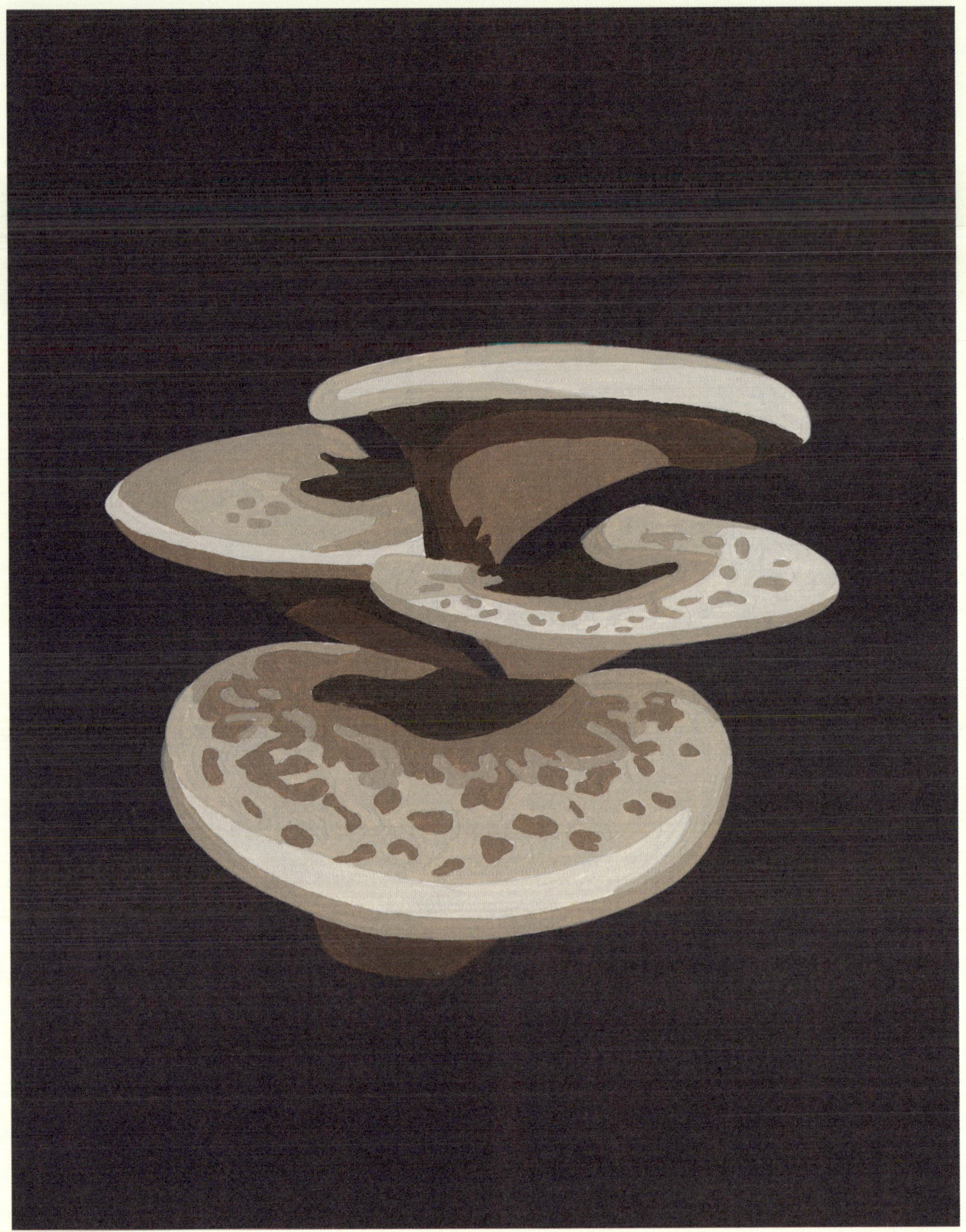

DRYAD'S SADDLE

Polyporus squamosus

DRYAD'S SADDLE

POLYPORUS SQUAMOSUS

EAT THE YOUNG

Can a mushroom taste like a watermelon? Well, this one can, as long as you eat it when it's pretty young. (Just be sure to cook it first.) If you wait until it matures, it gets inedibly tough and leathery (as we all do when we age). This top-heavy mushie has a wide, flat cap, which sometimes grows so big that it falls over on itself and detaches from the tree it's growing on.

The backstory about this mushroom's name is a fun one: It comes from a Greek myth about dryads—or tree nymphs—that are tiny enough to ride these 'shrooms like saddles. I can just see those little sprites zooming around on these saucer caps. Besides the shape, this fungus is pretty easy to identify because of the brown scalelike pattern on their caps and the fact that they don't have gills. They grow on dead trees (or trees that are dying) right after a good rain in the early spring.

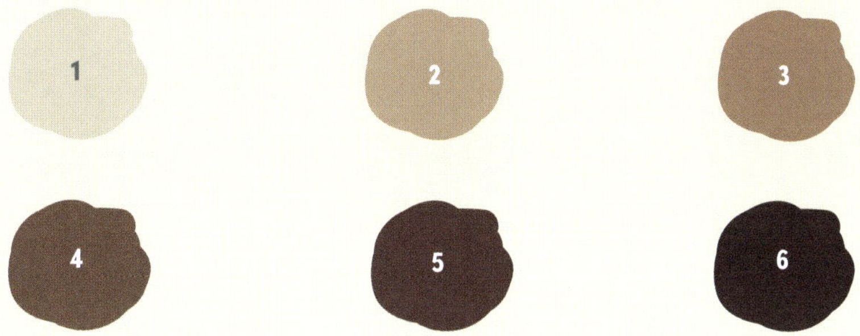

TO BLEND YOUR OWN COLORS FOR THIS PRINT, SEE PAGE 111 FOR BLENDING RECIPES AND SWATCH SAMPLES.

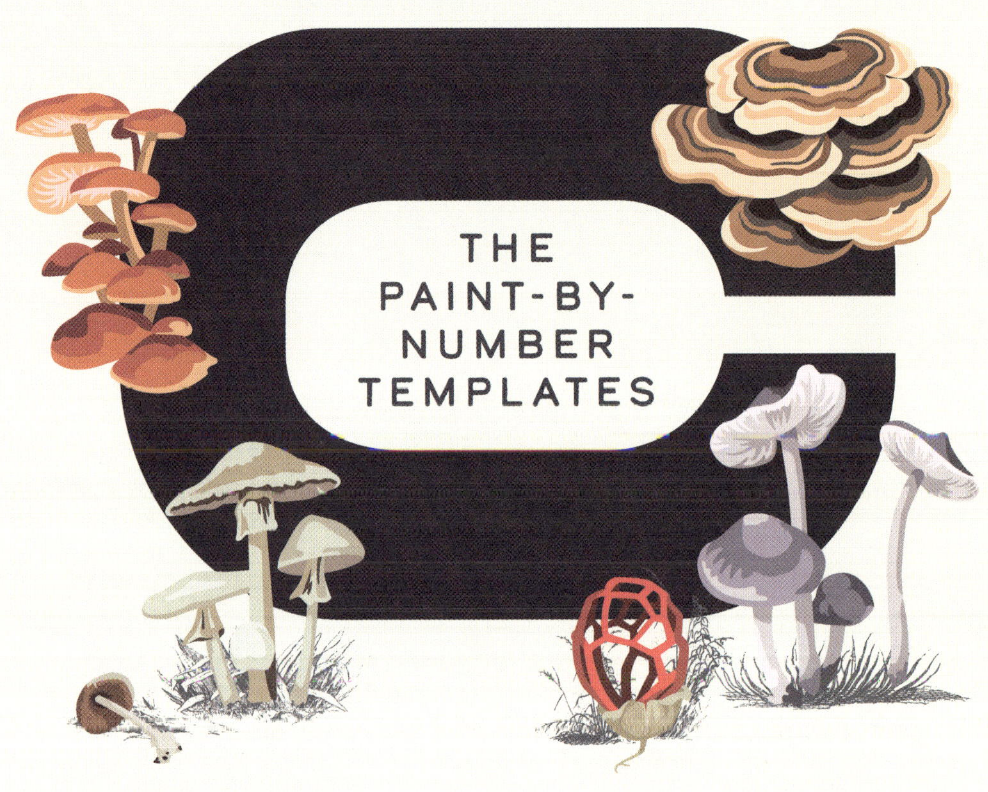

THE PAINT-BY-NUMBER TEMPLATES

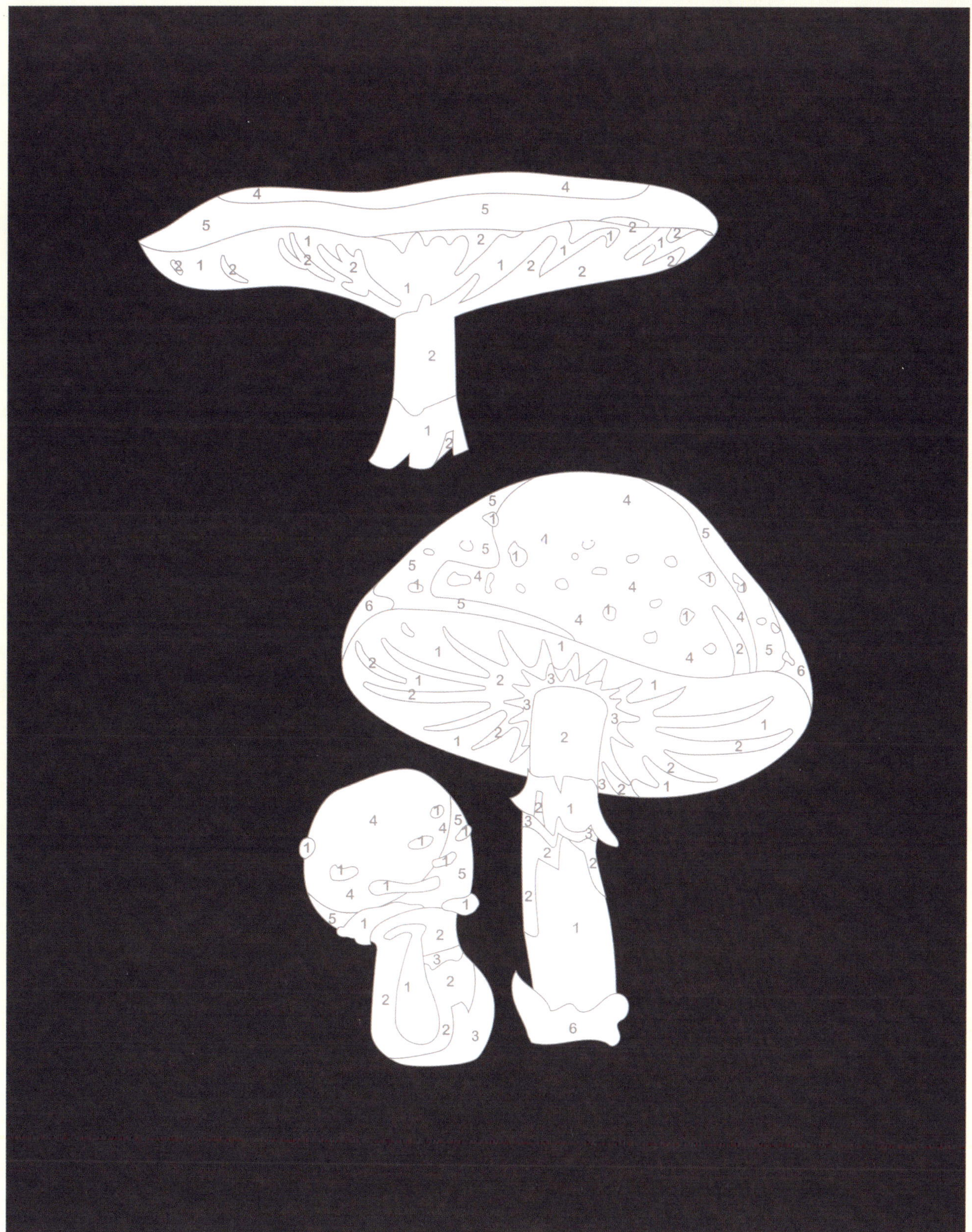
FLY AGARIC
Amanita muscaria

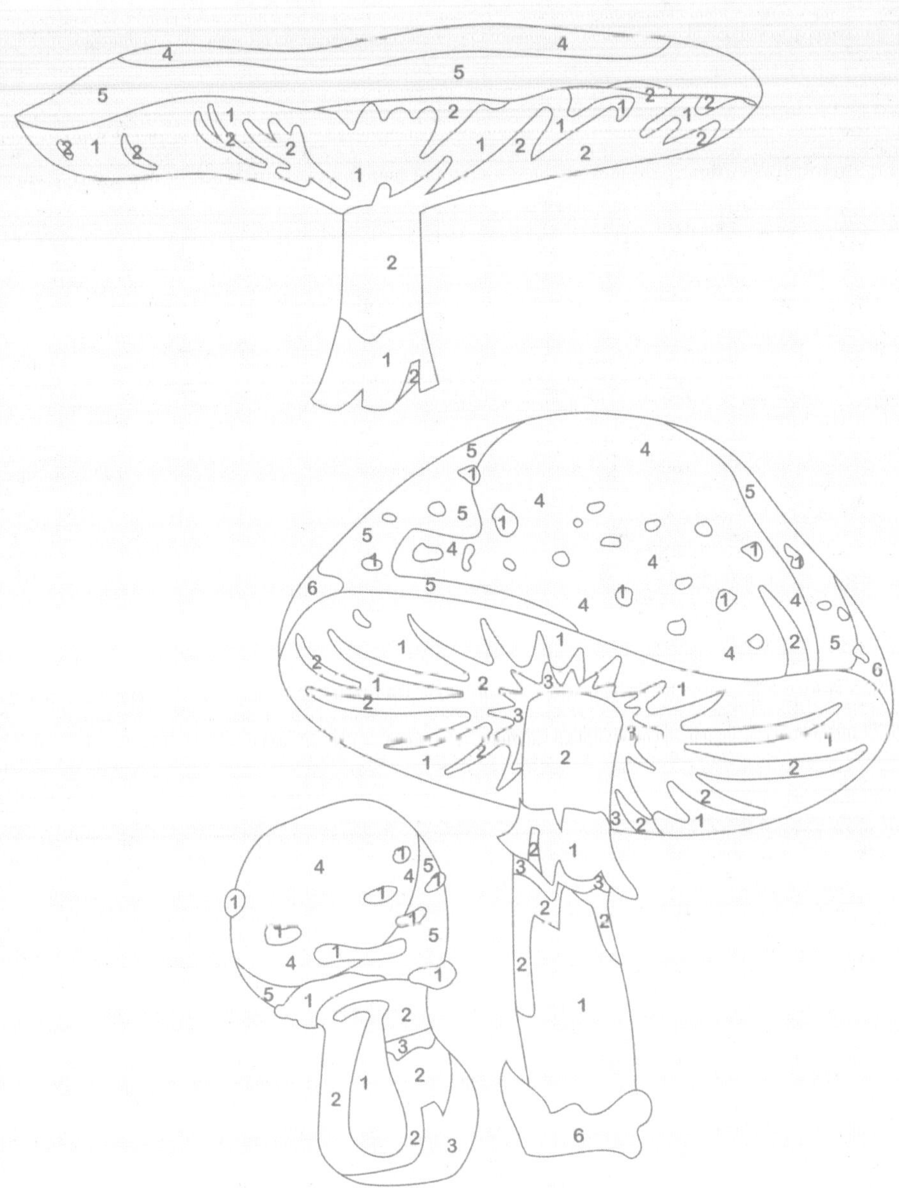

FLY AGARIC

Amanita muscaria

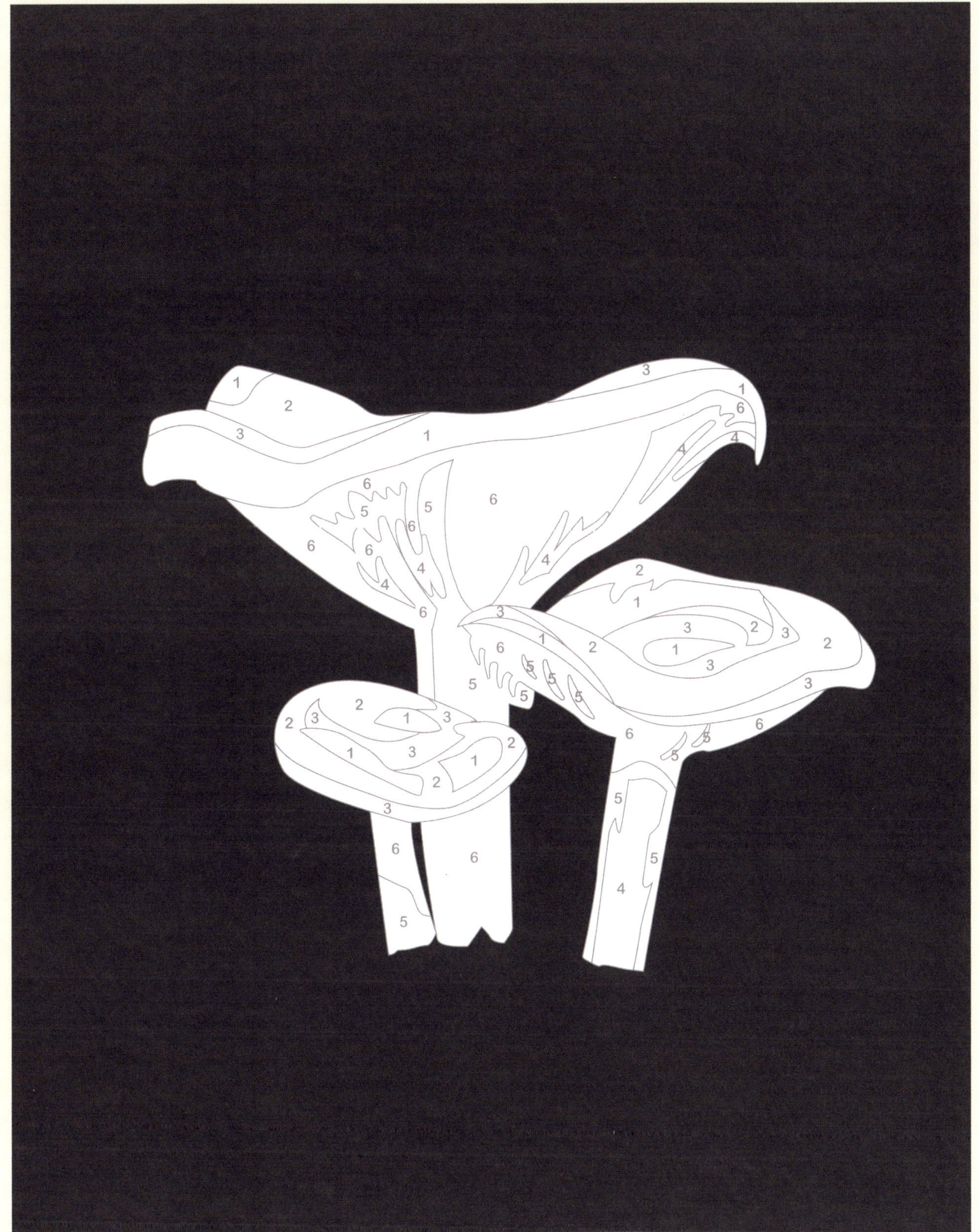

ANISEED TOADSTOOL

Clitocybe odora

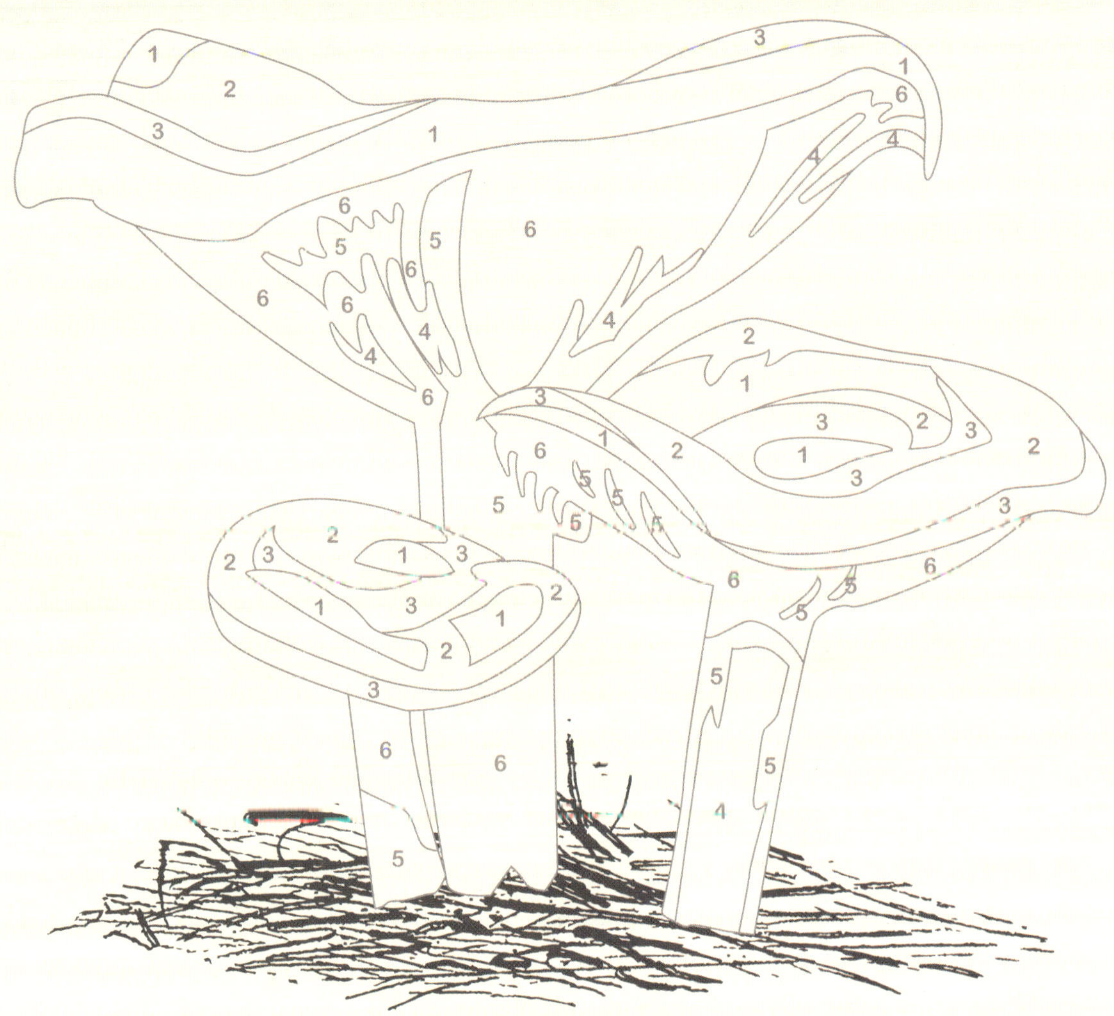

ANISEED TOADSTOOL

Clitocybe odora

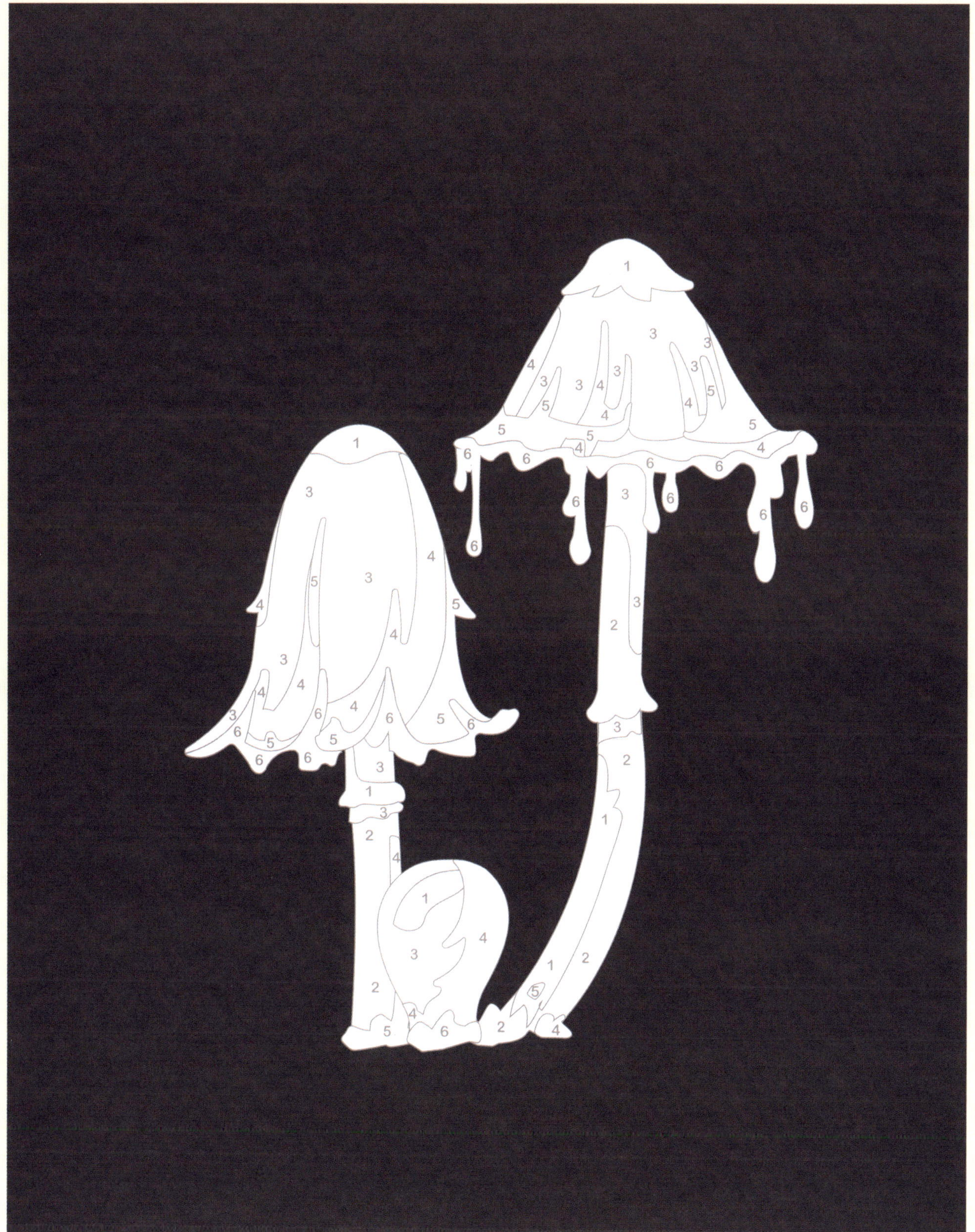

INKY CAP

Coprinopsis atramentaria

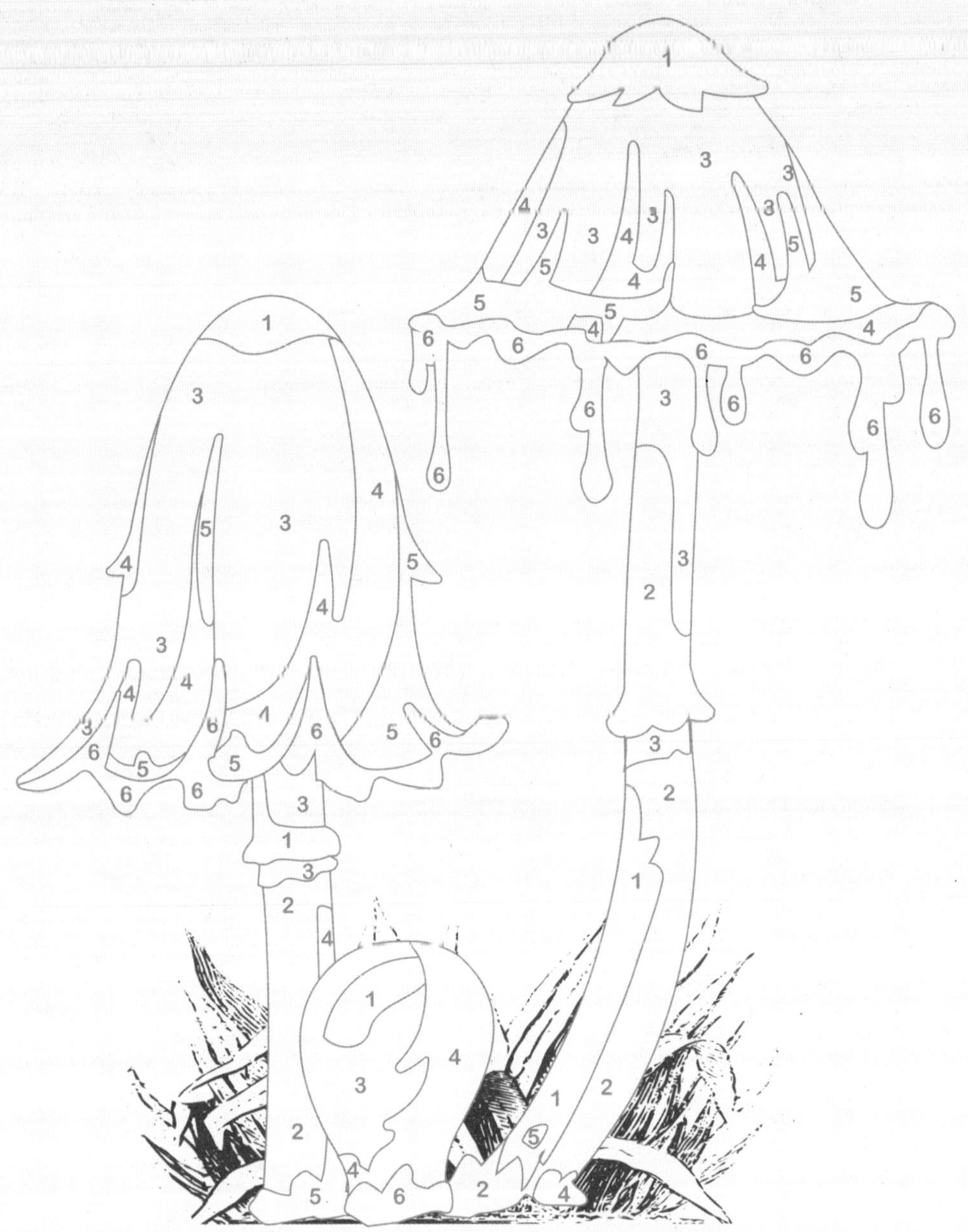

INKY CAP

Coprinopsis atramentaria

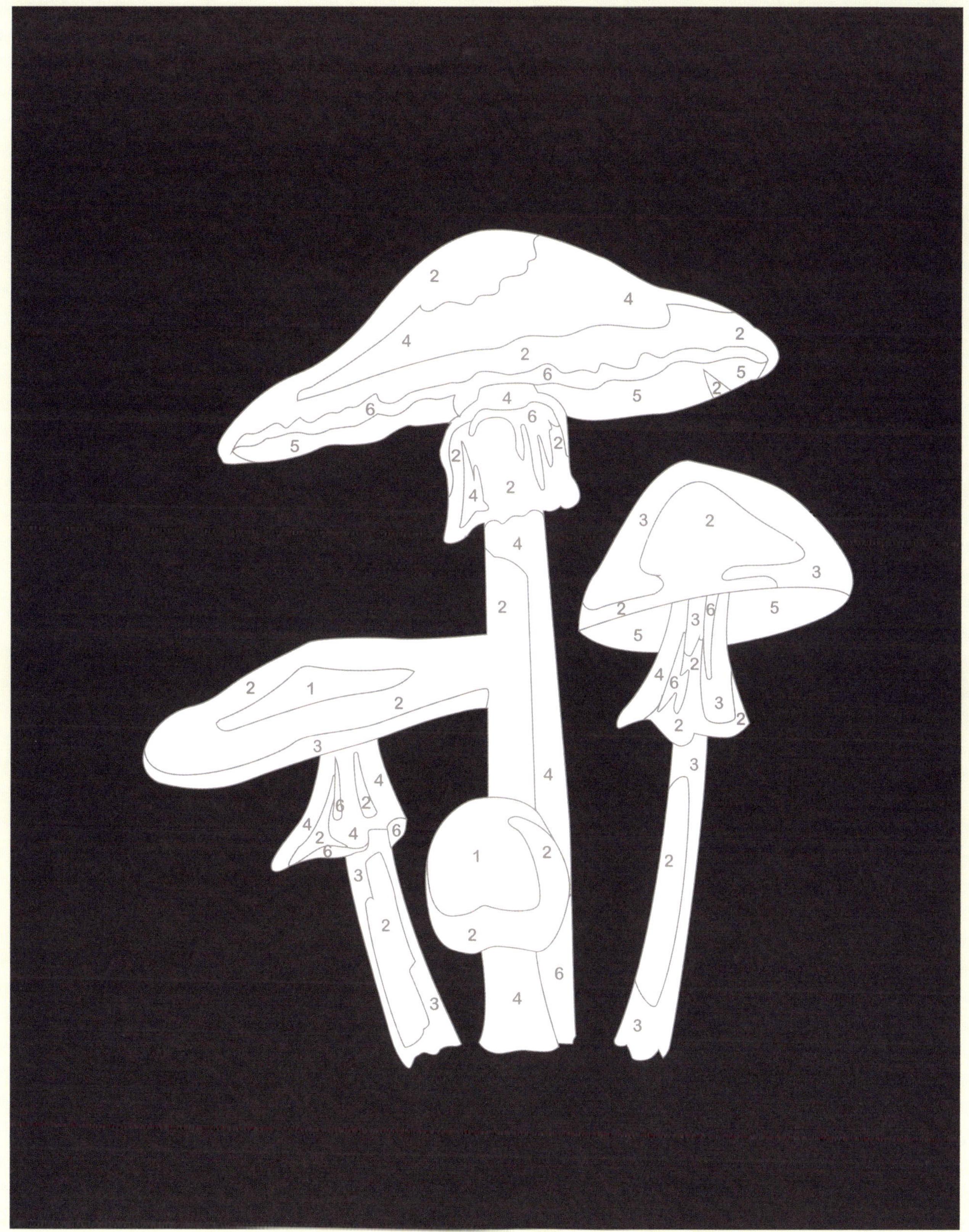

DESTROYING ANGEL

Amanita virosa

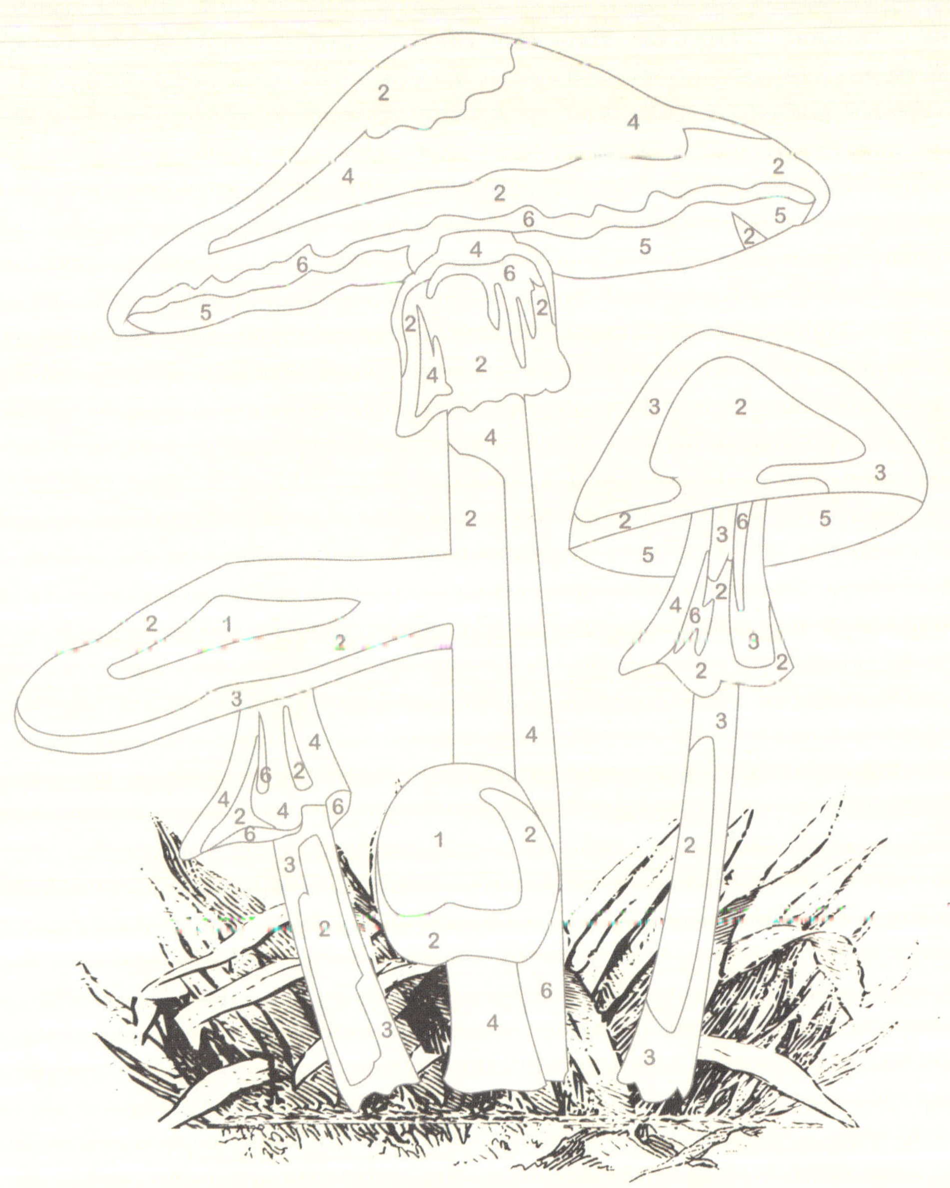

DESTROYING ANGEL

Amanita virosa

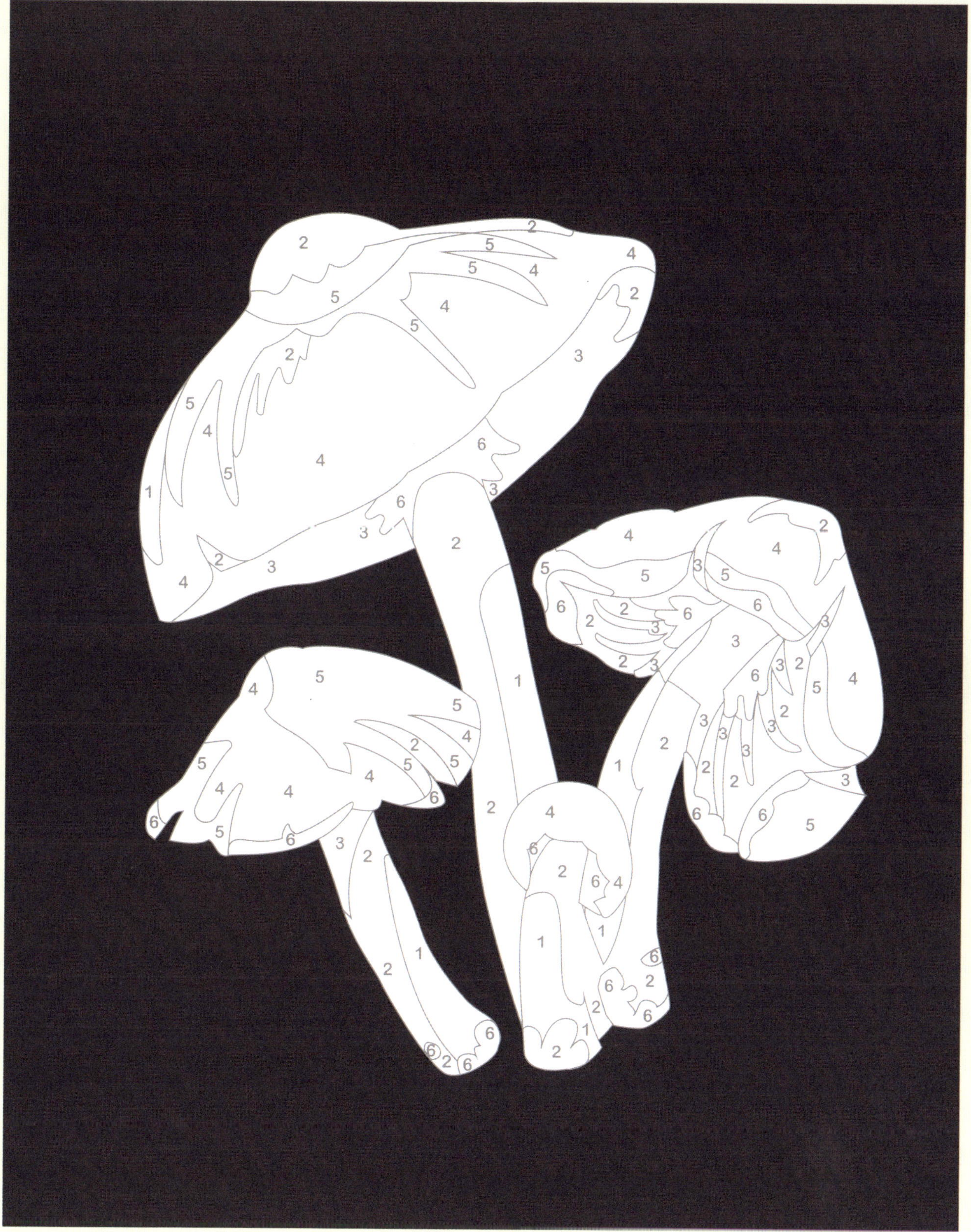

DEADLY FIBRECAP

Inocybe erubescens

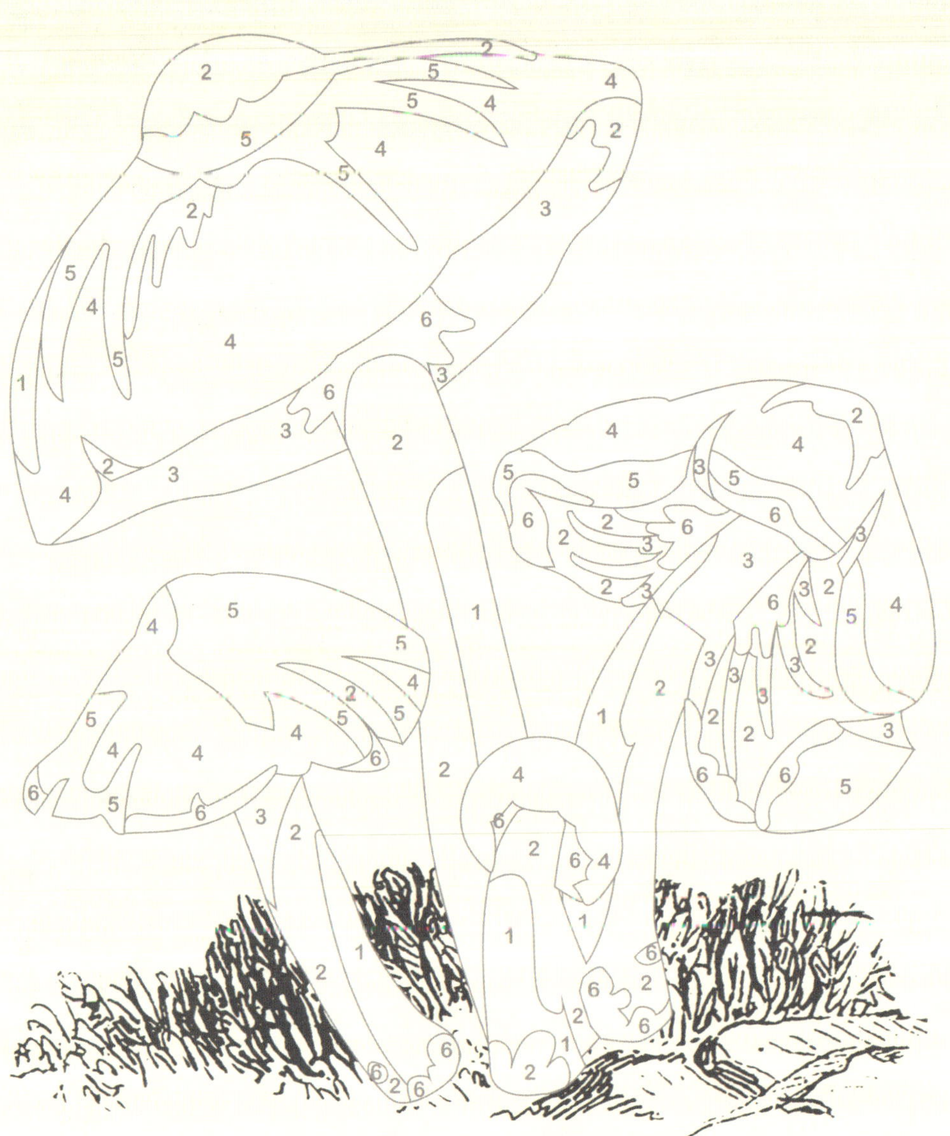

DEADLY FIBRECAP

Inocybe erubescens

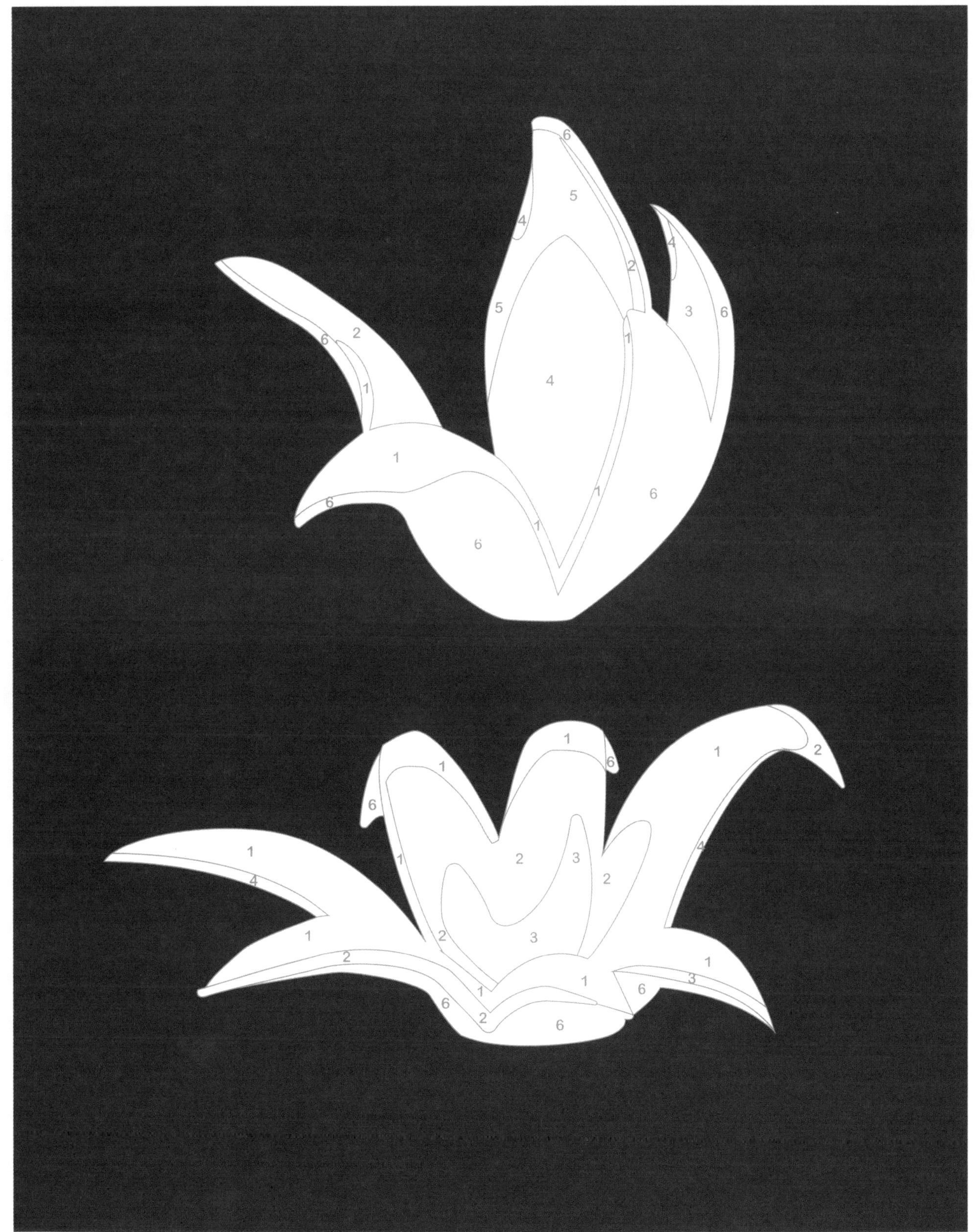

DEVIL'S CIGAR

Chorioactis geaster

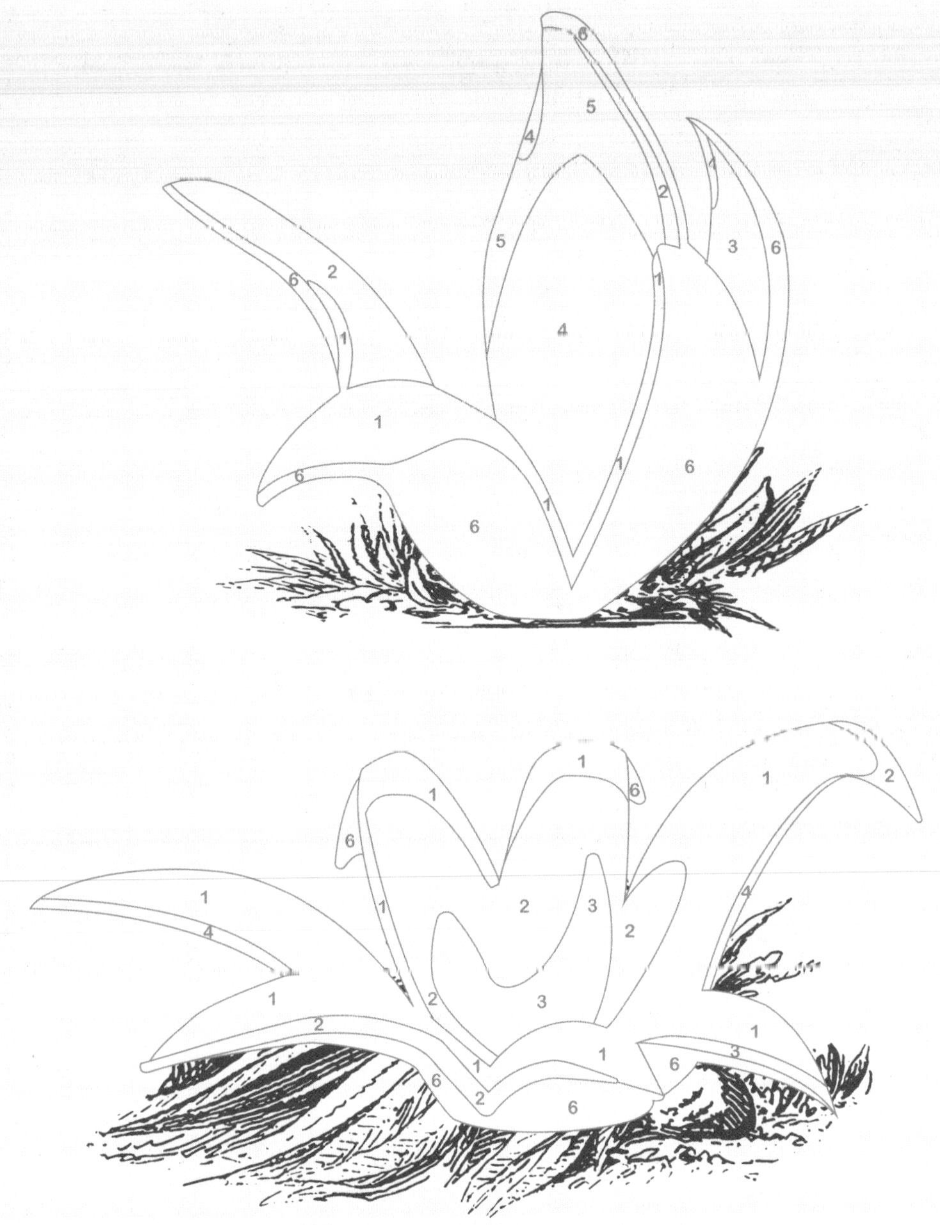

DEVIL'S CIGAR

Chorioactis geaster

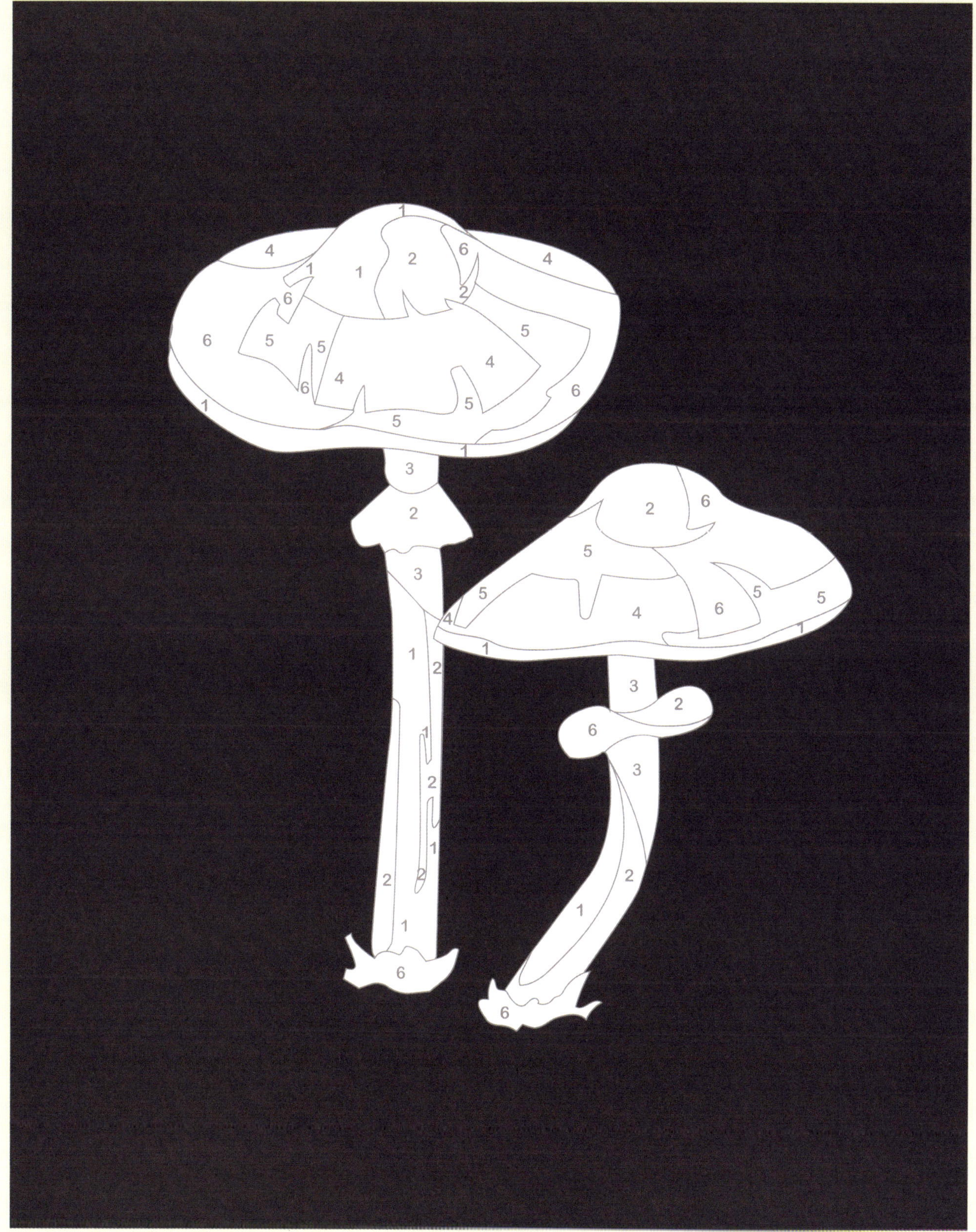

VERDIGRIS AGARIC

Stropharia aeruginosa

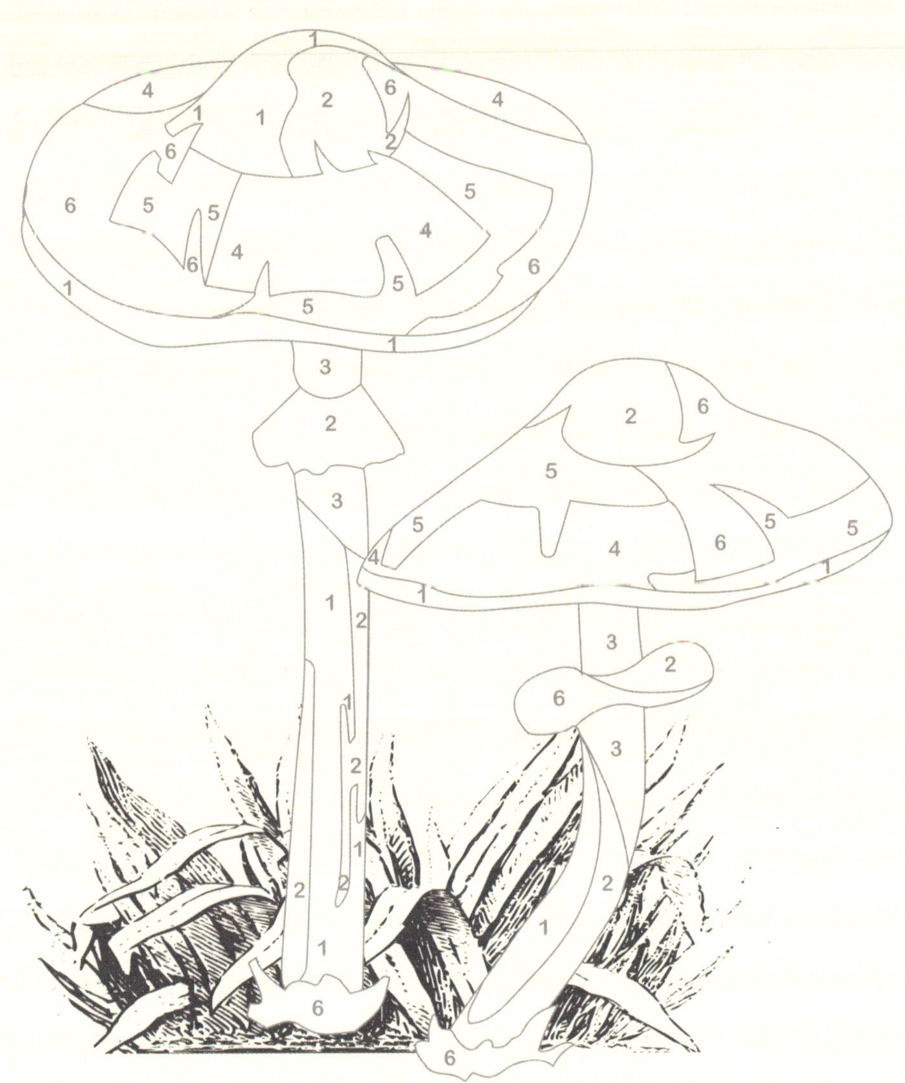

VERDIGRIS AGARIC

Stropharia aeruginosa

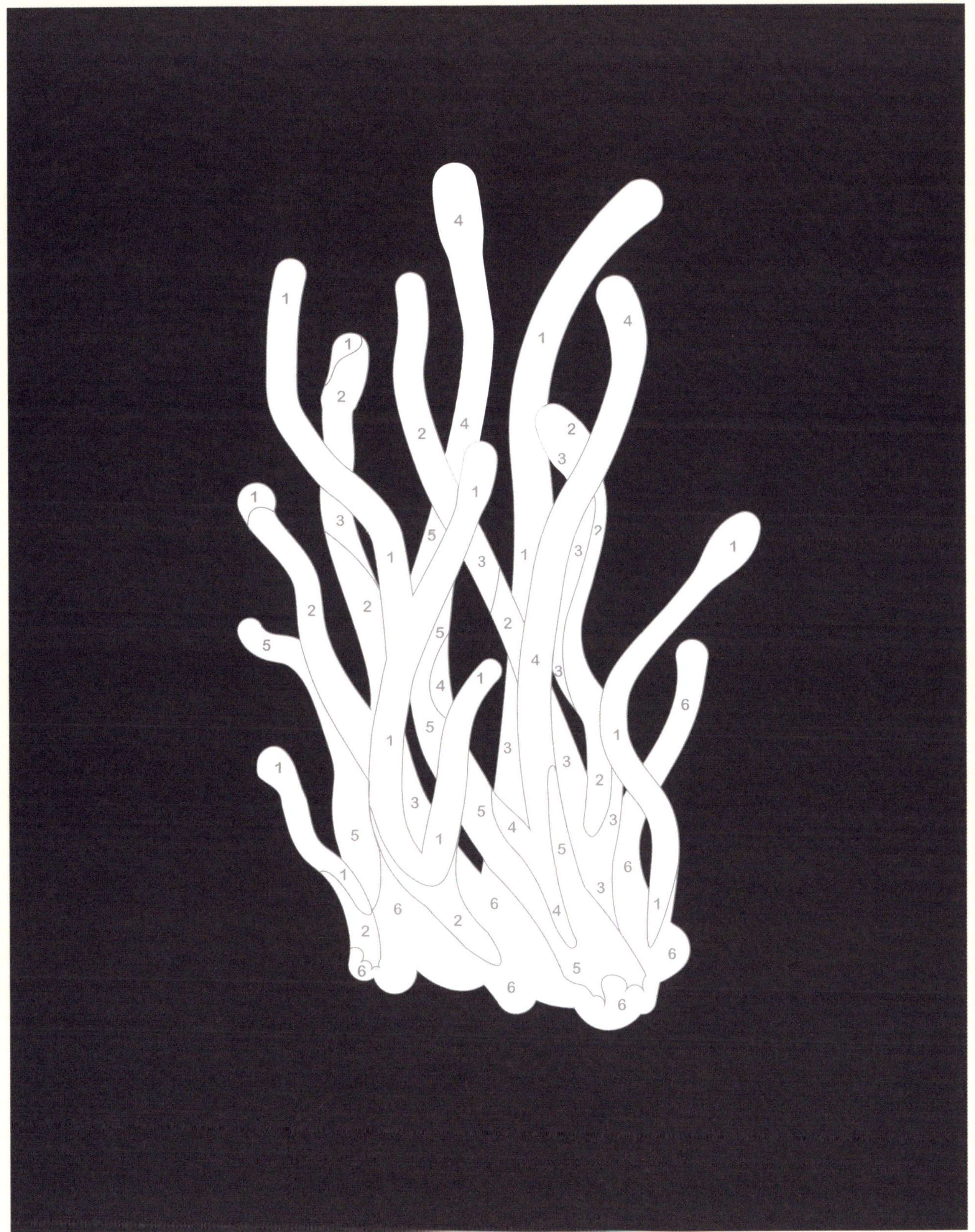

SCARLET CATERPILLAR CLUB

Cordyceps militaris

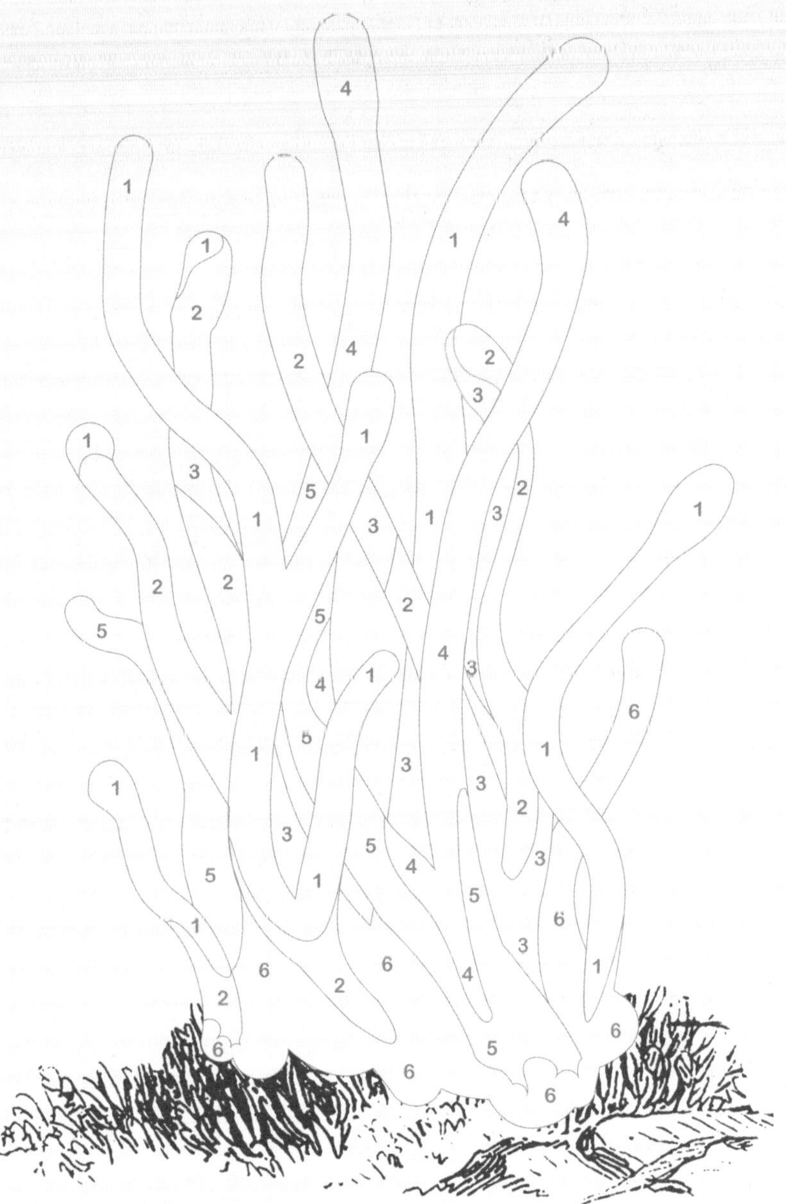

SCARLET CATERPILLAR CLUB

Cordyceps militaris

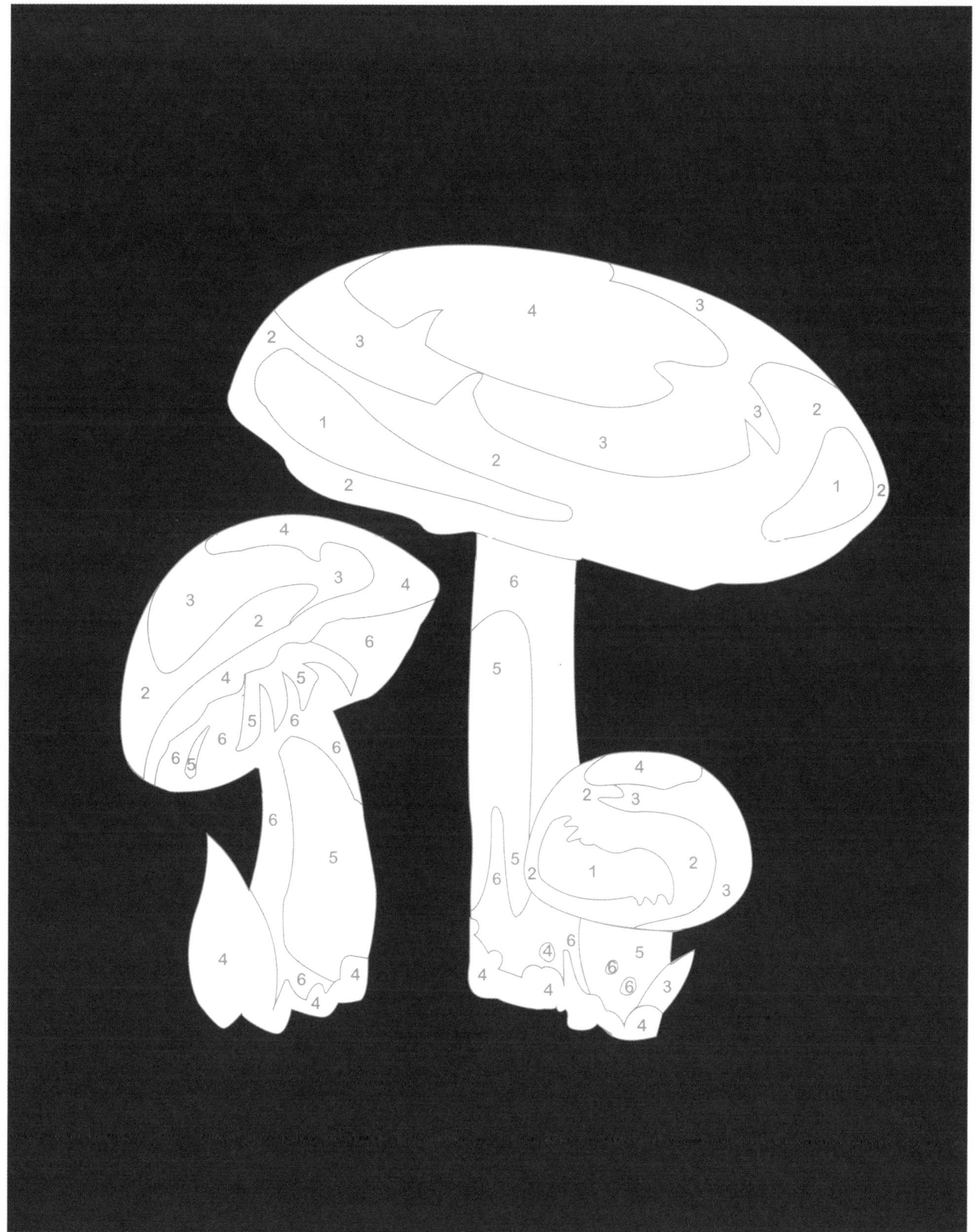

DEATH CAP

Amanita phalloides

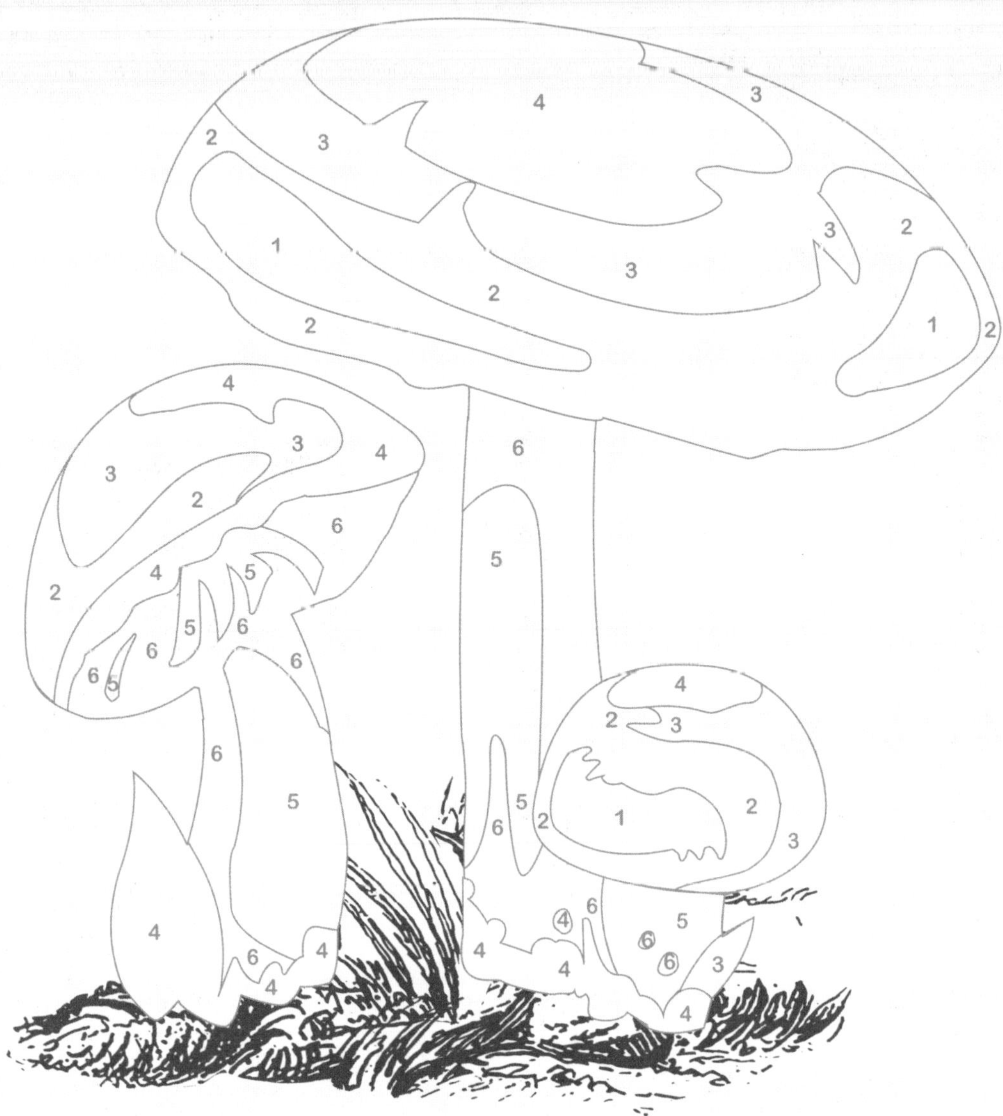

DEATH CAP

Amanita phalloides

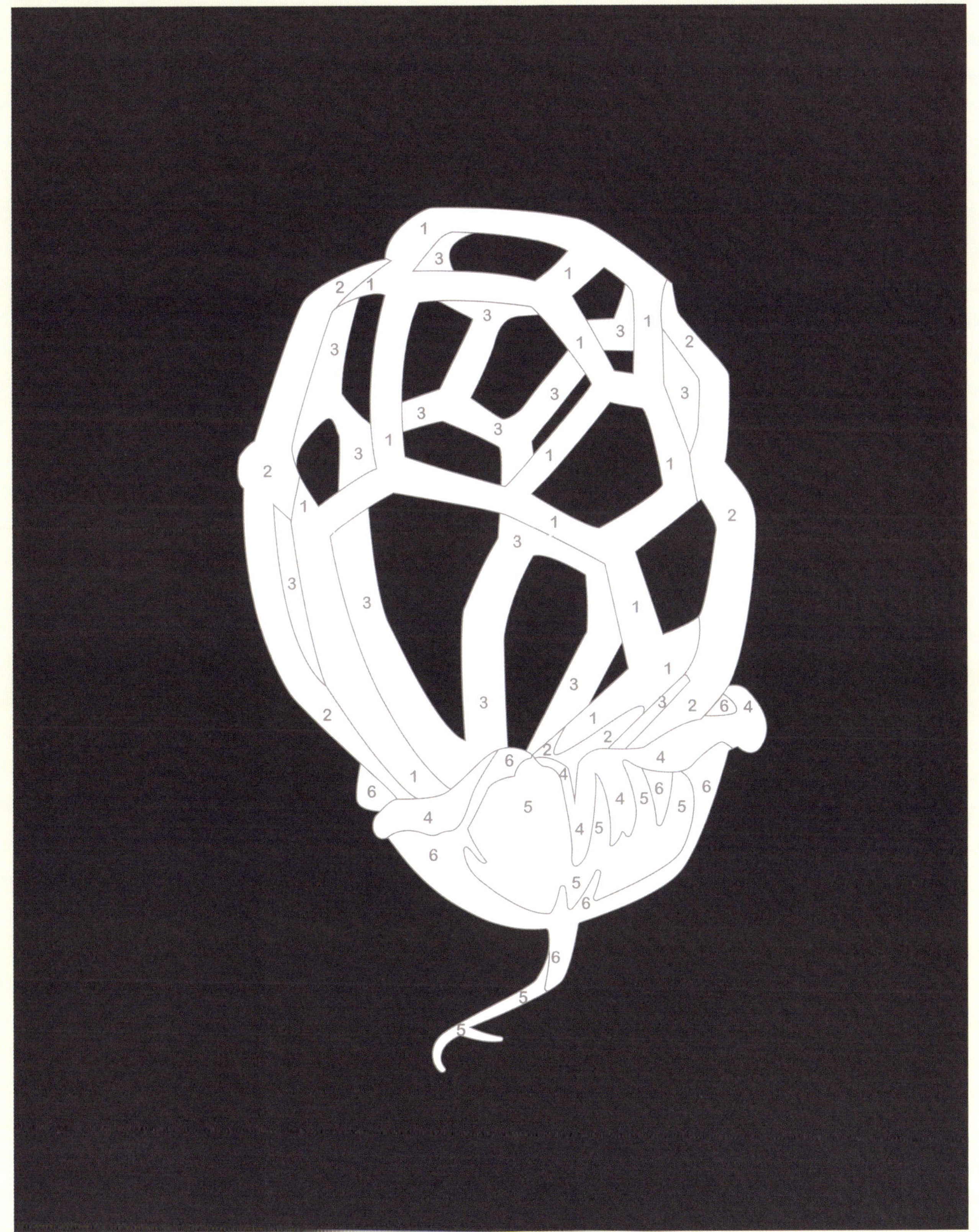

LATTICED STINKHORN

Clathrus ruber

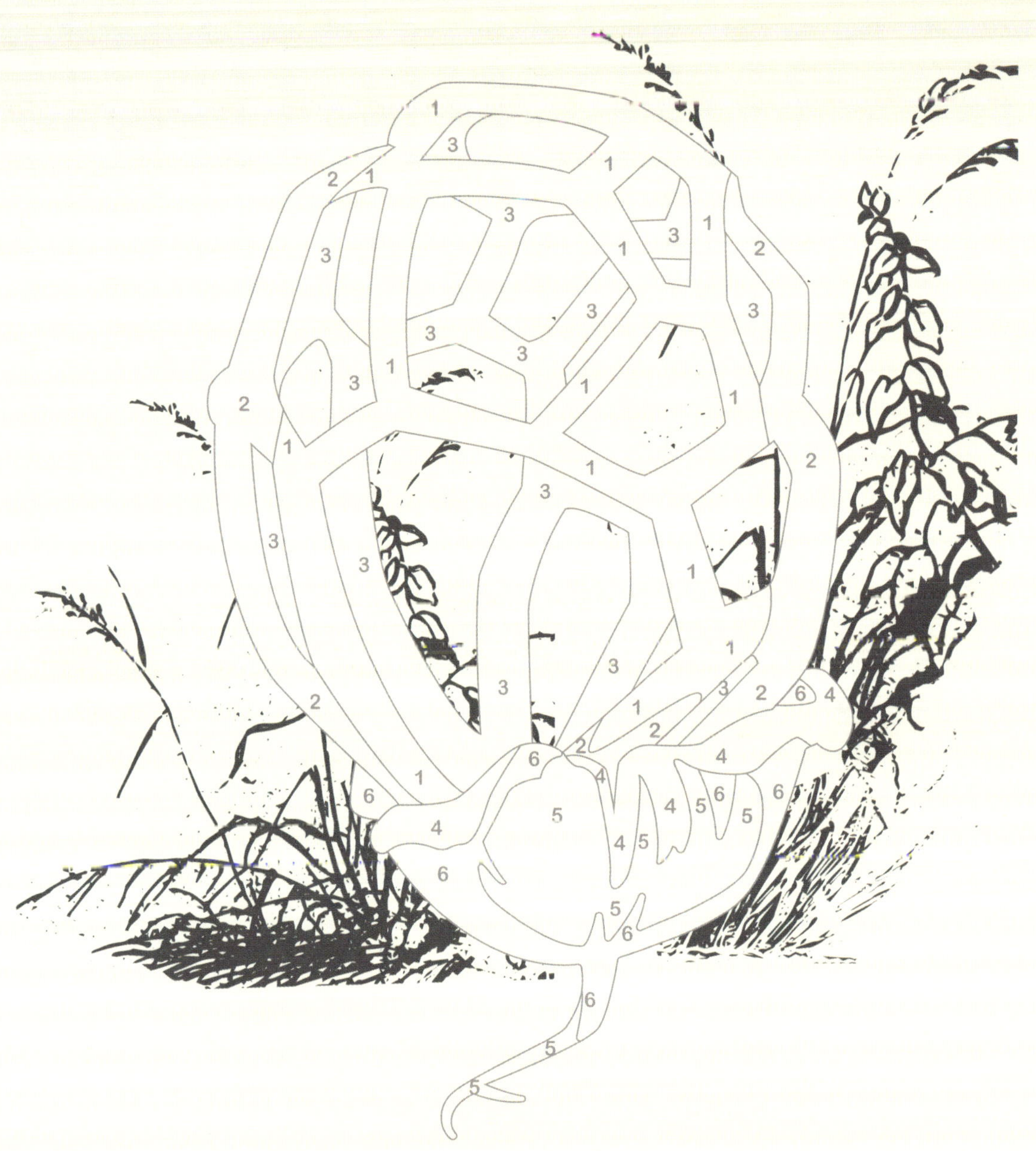

LATTICED STINKHORN

Clathrus ruber

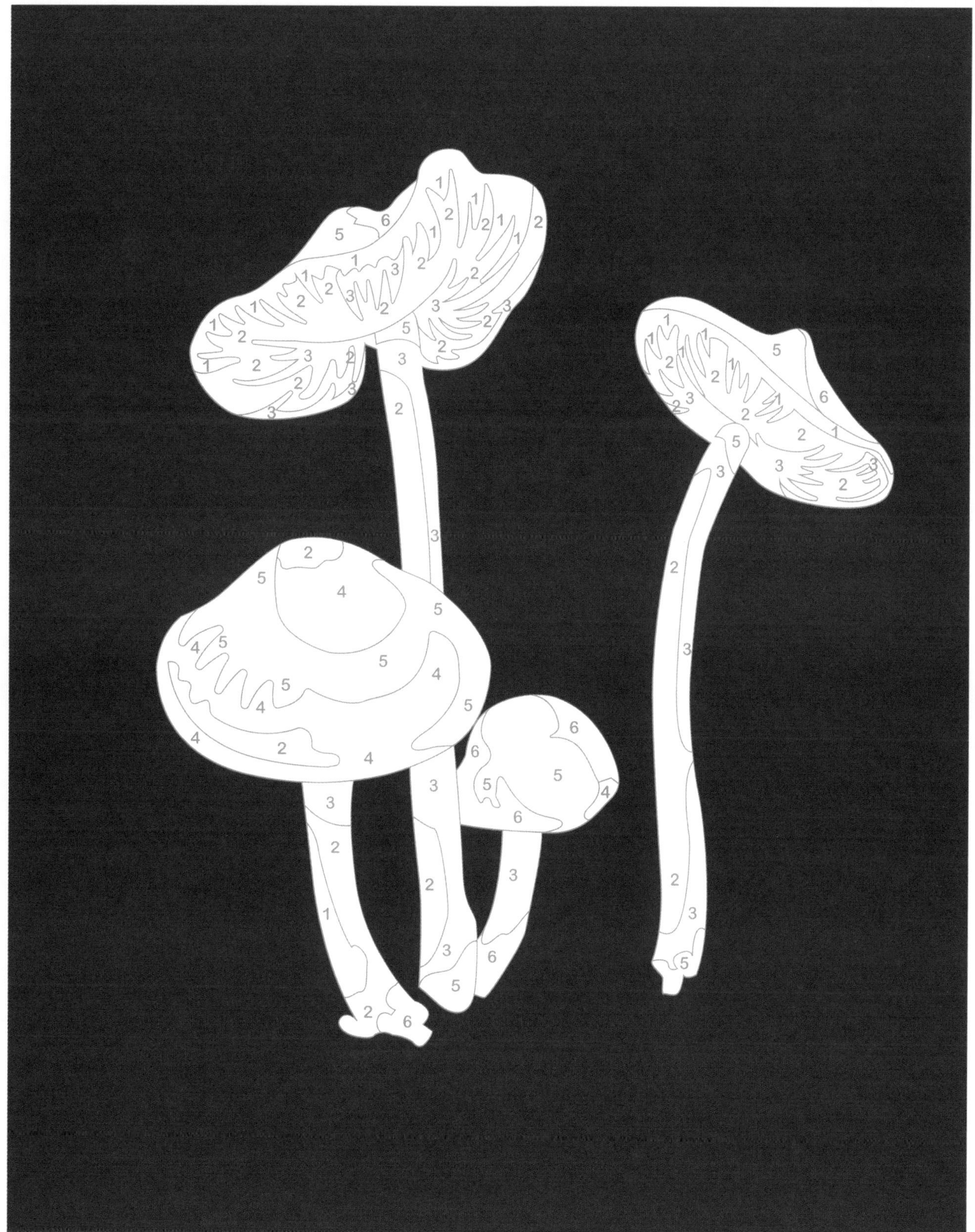

LILAC BONNET

Mycena pura

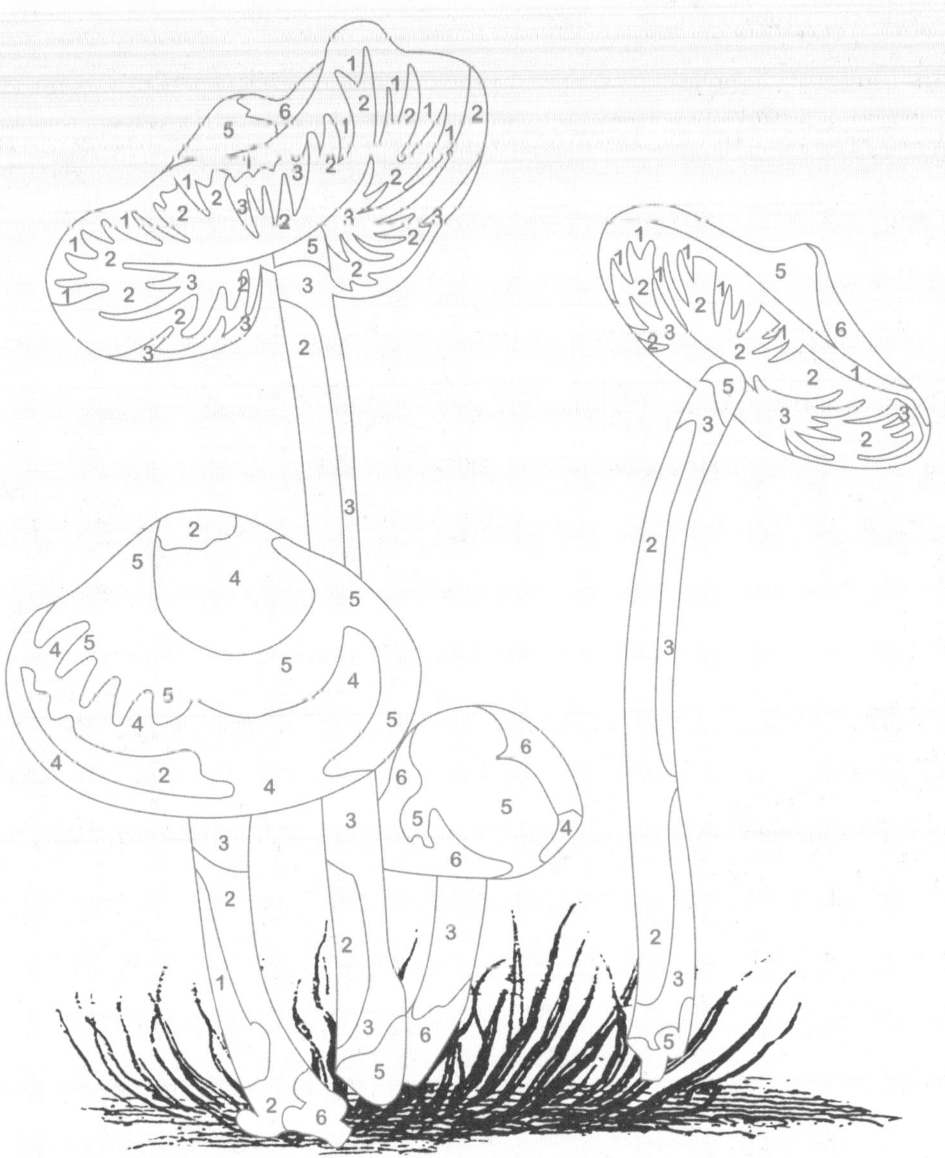

LILAC BONNET

Mycena pura

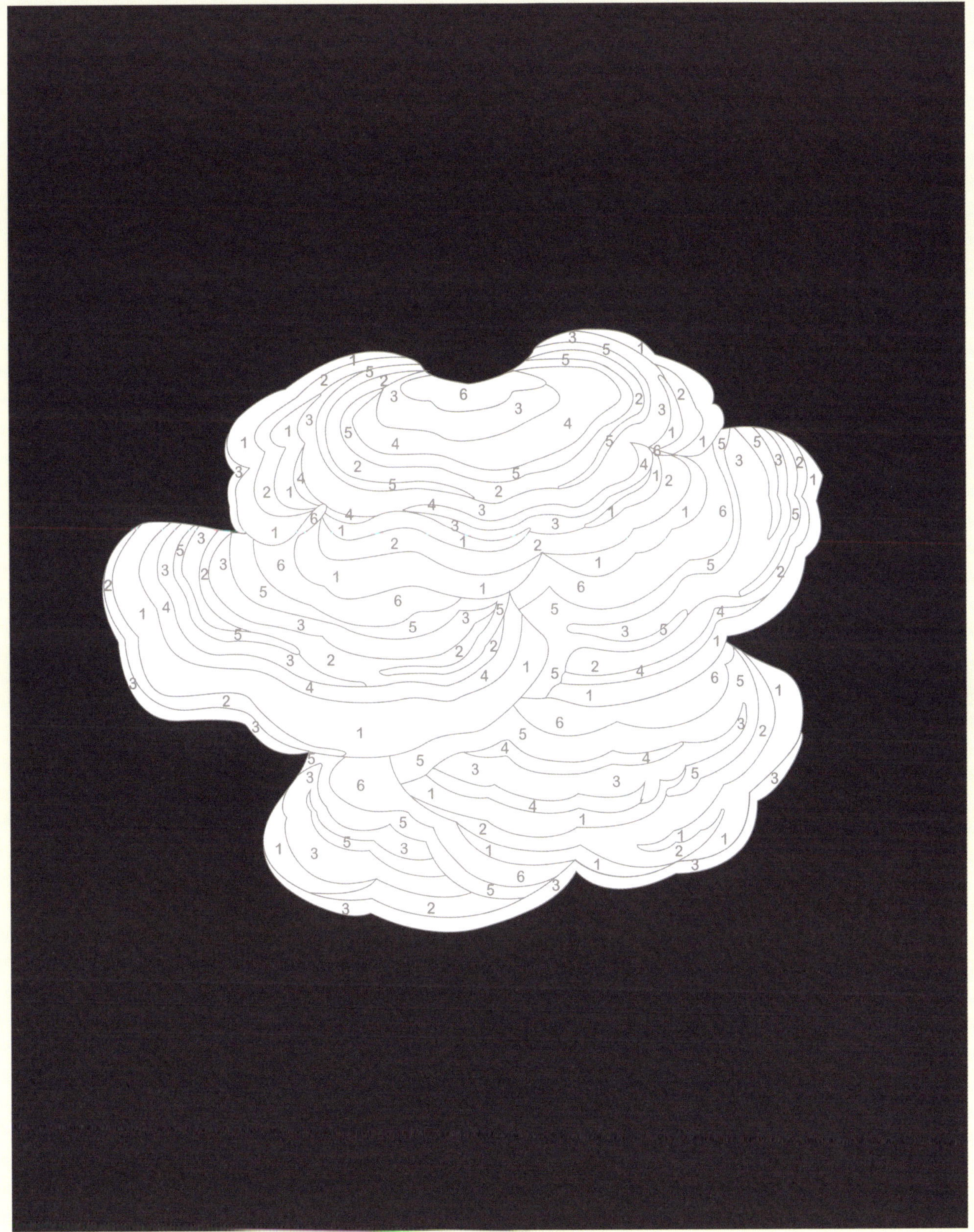

TURKEY TAIL

Trametes versicolor

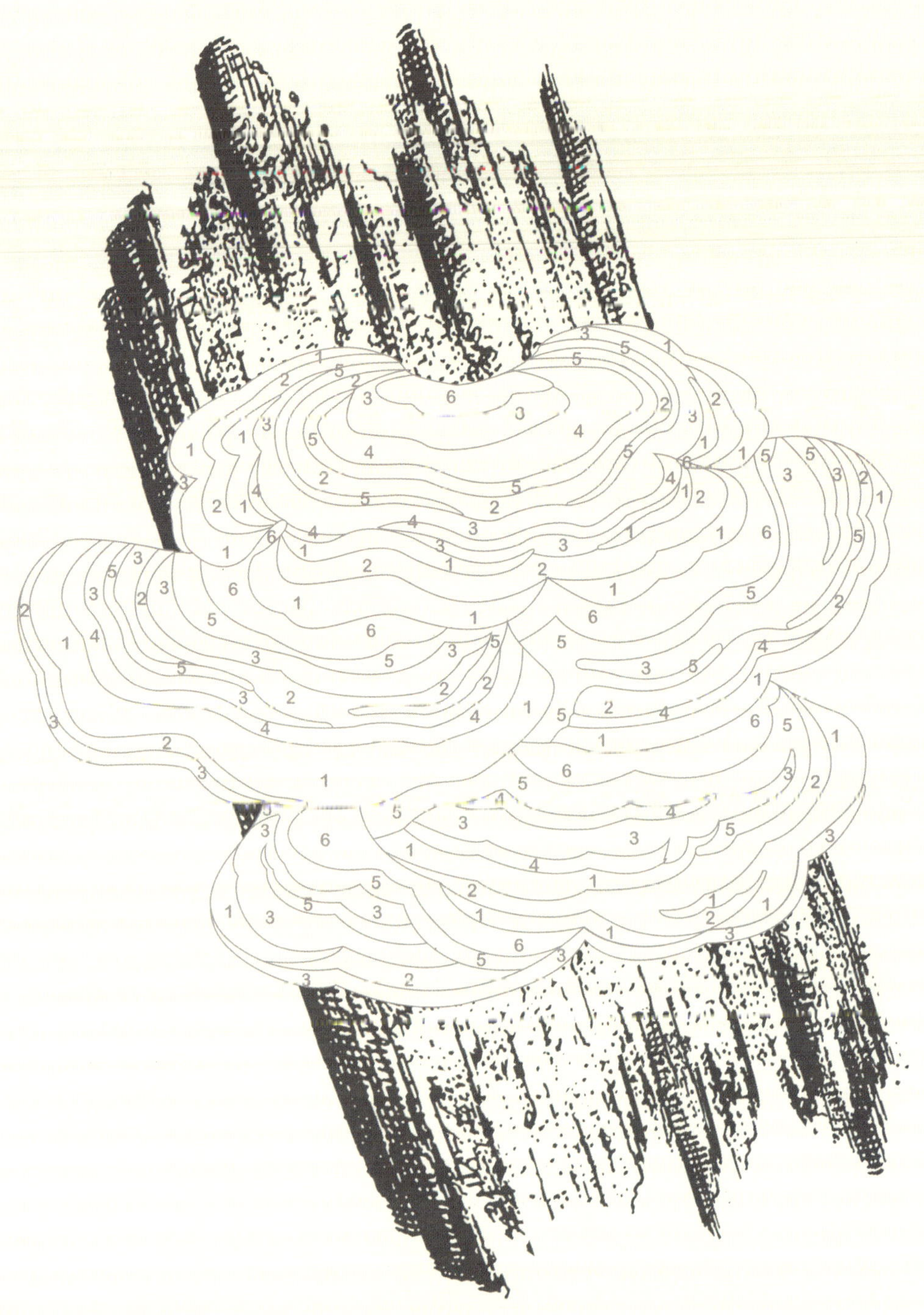

TURKEY TAIL

Trametes versicolor

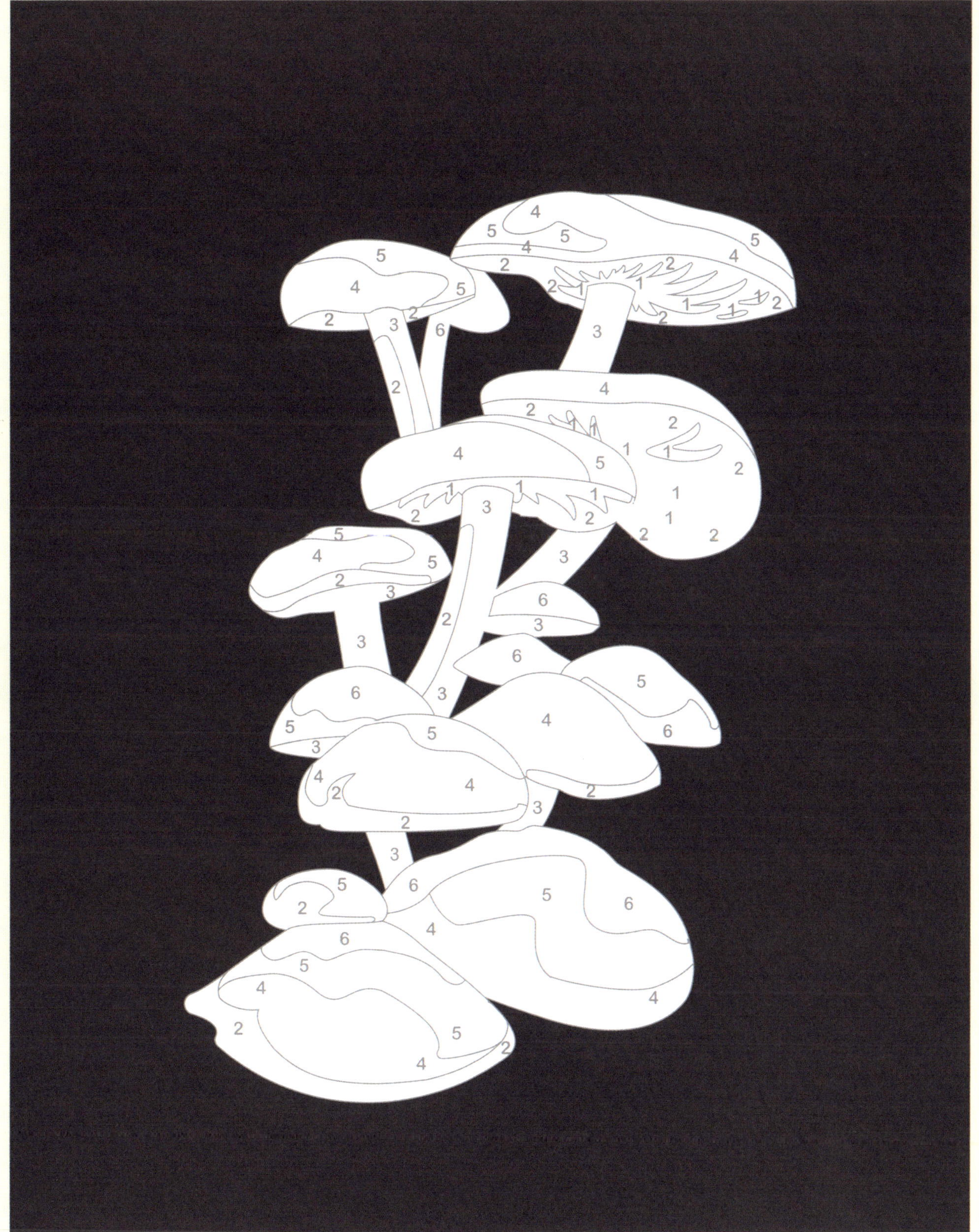

VELVET SHANK

Flammulina velutipes

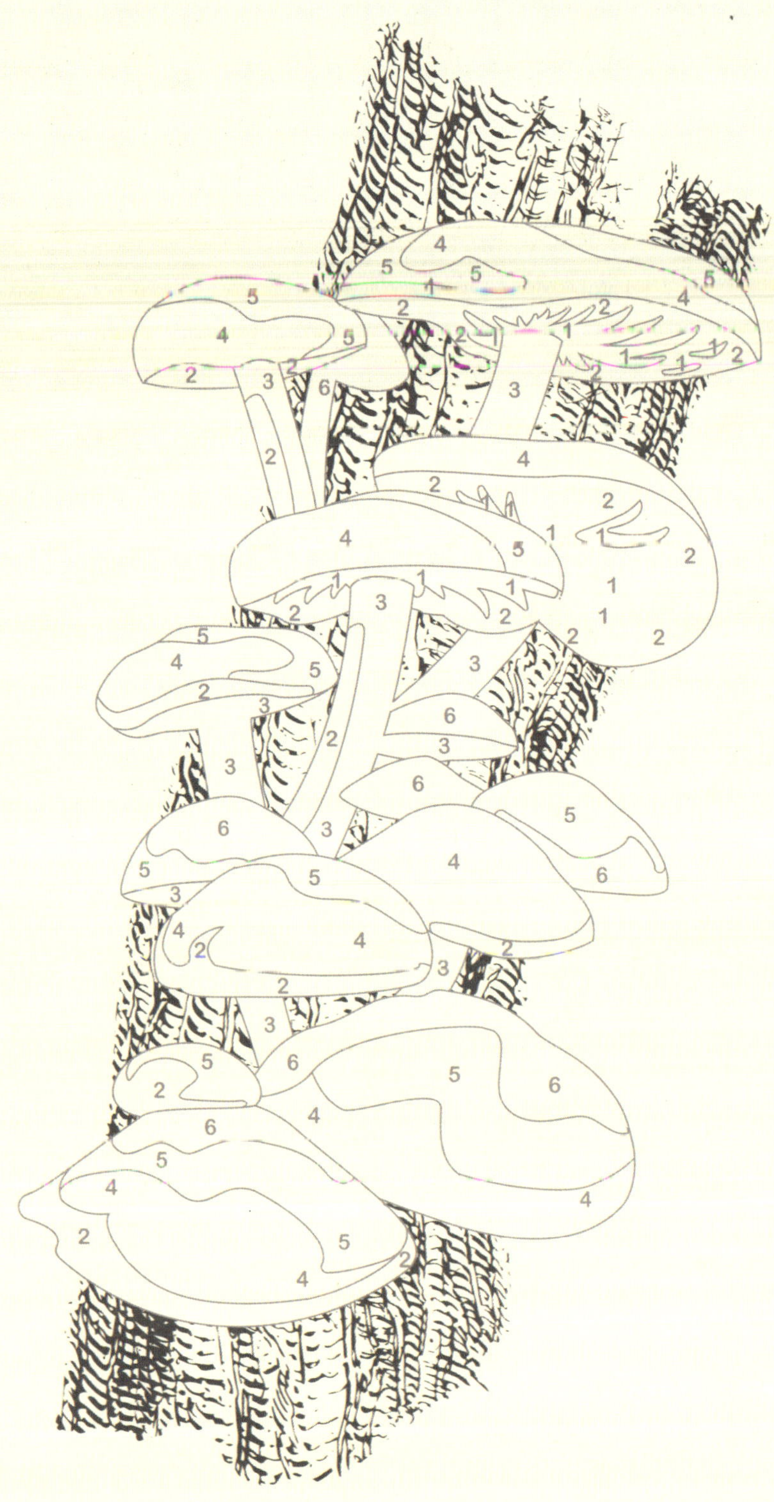

VELVET SHANK

Flammulina velutipes

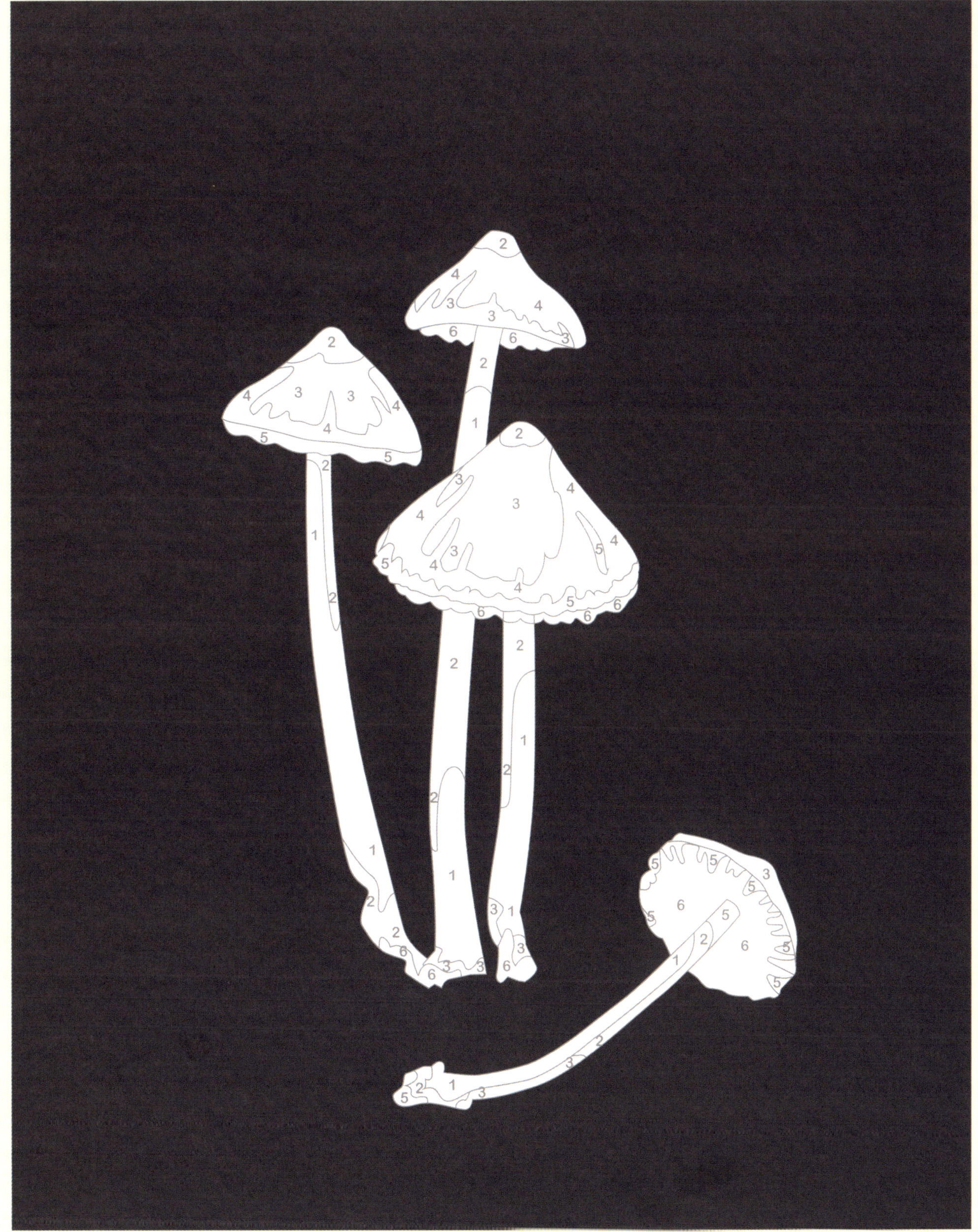

SKY-BLUE MUSHROOM

Entoloma hochstetteri

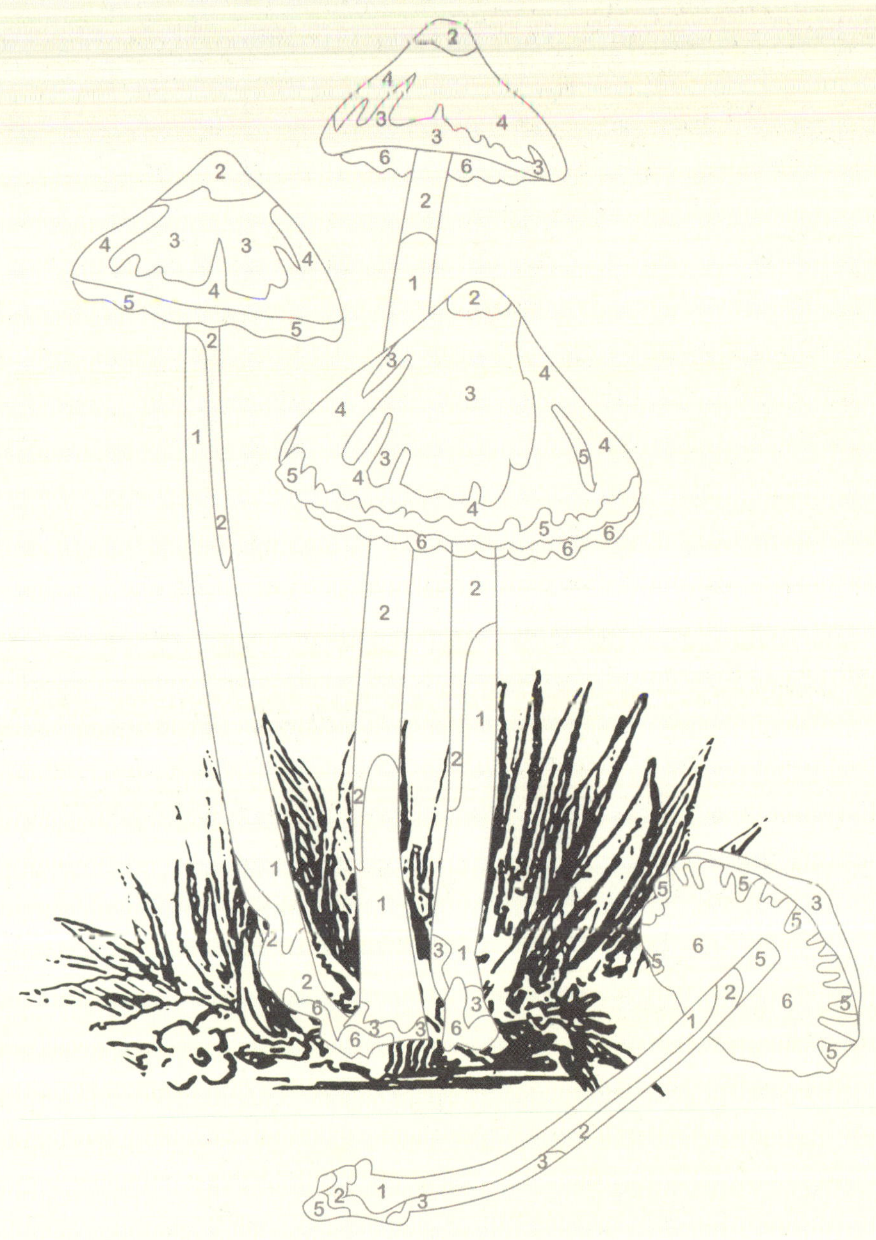

SKY-BLUE MUSHROOM
Entoloma hochstetteri

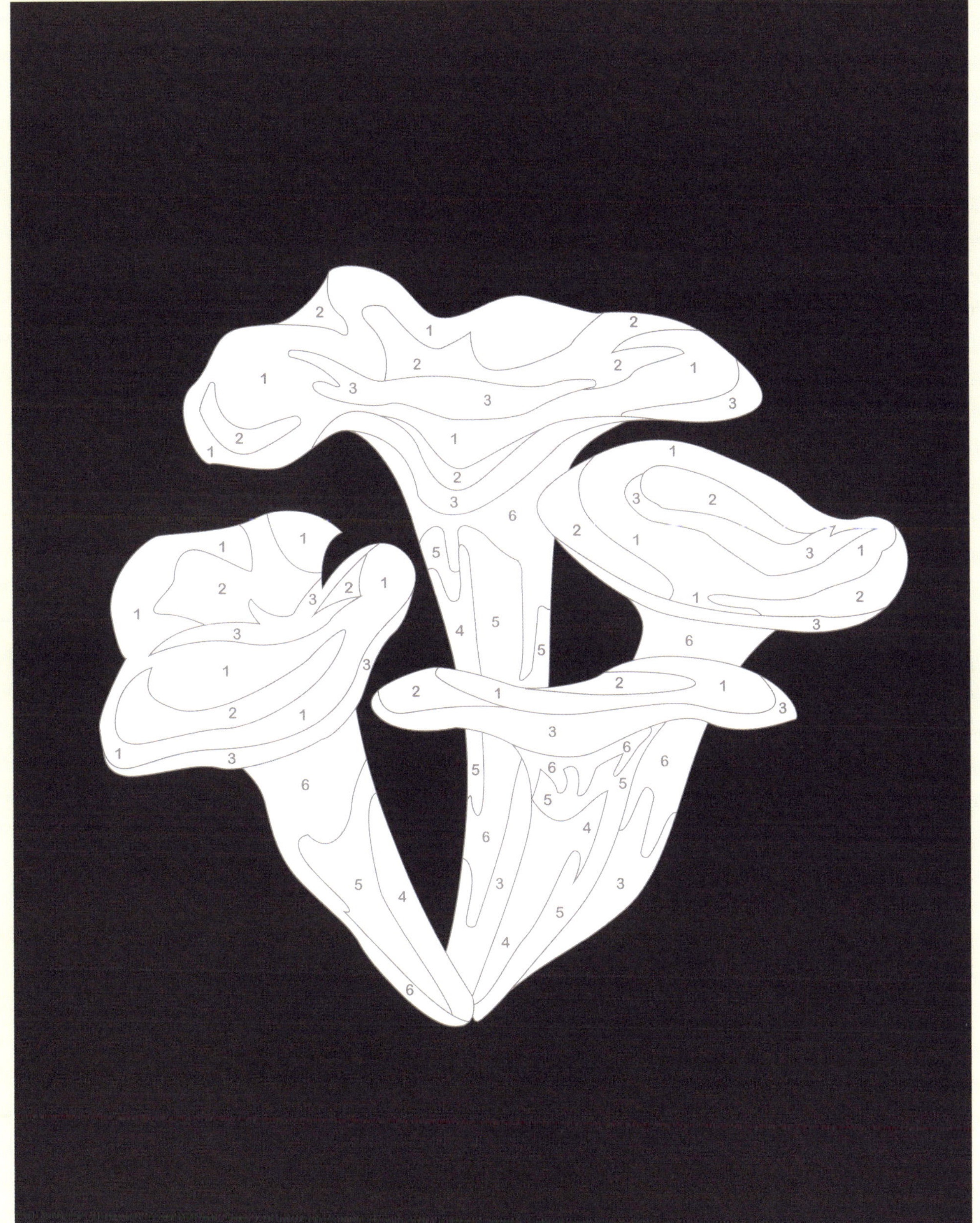

BLACK TRUMPET

Craterellus cornucopioides

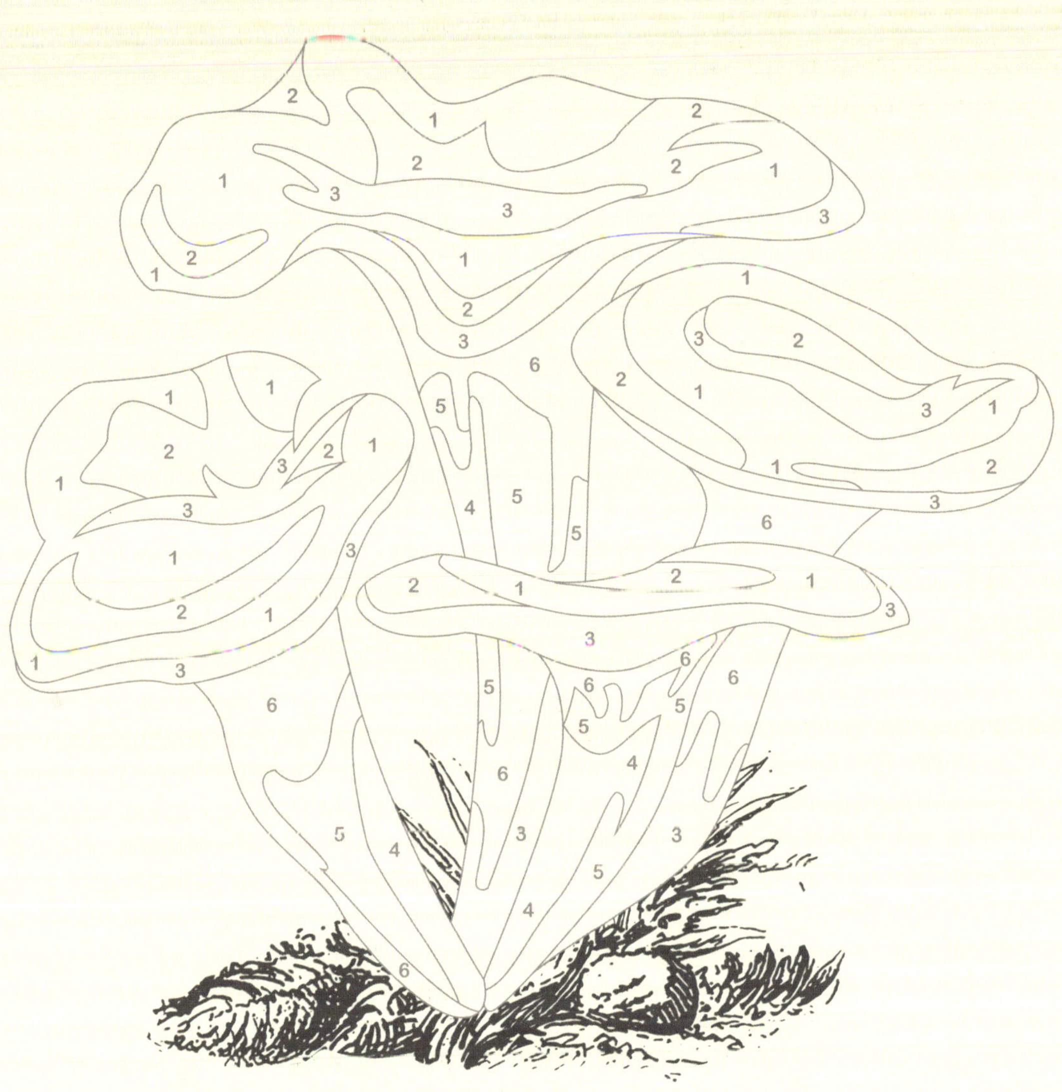

BLACK TRUMPET

Craterellus cornucopioides

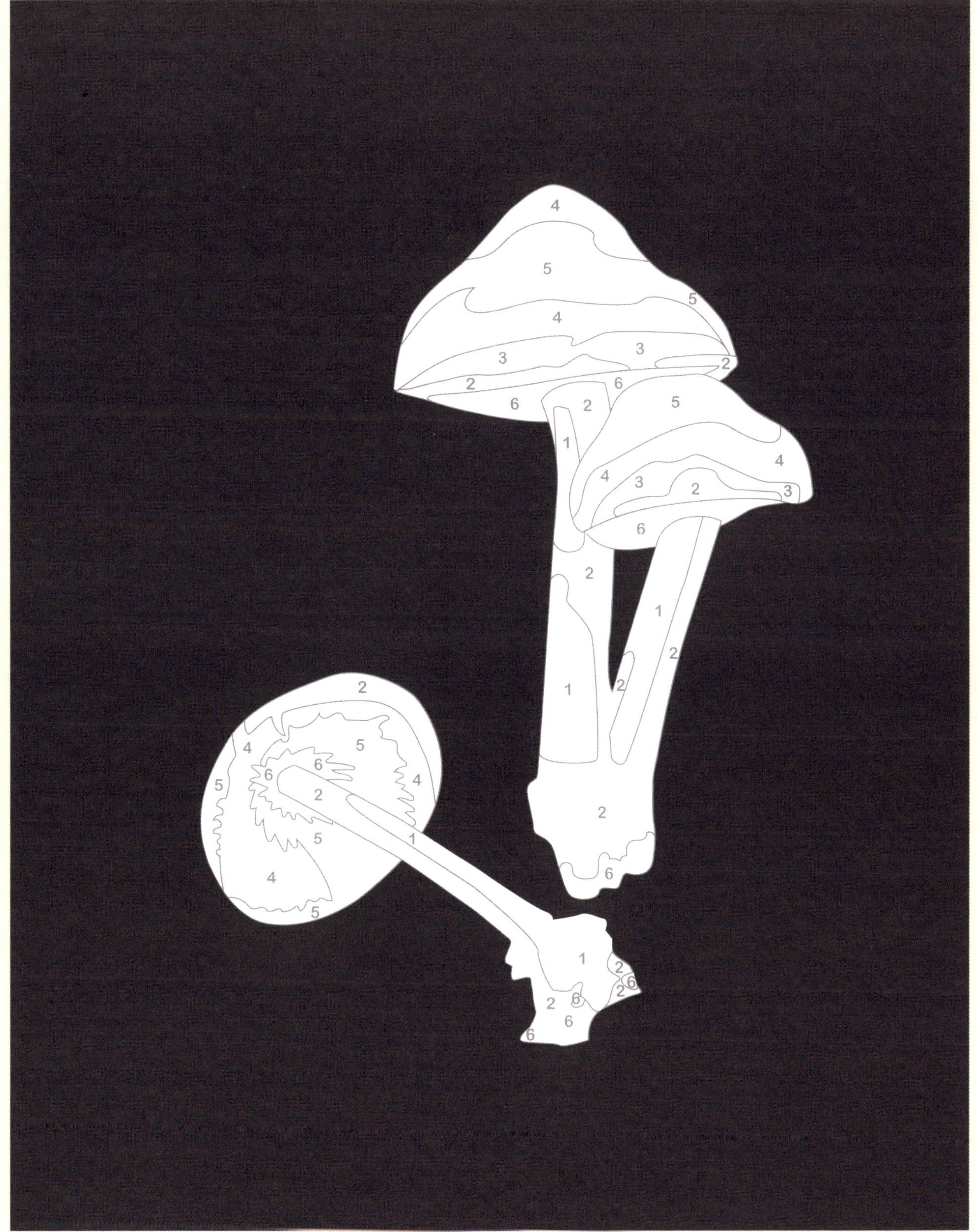

FLYING SAUCER

Psilocybe azurescens

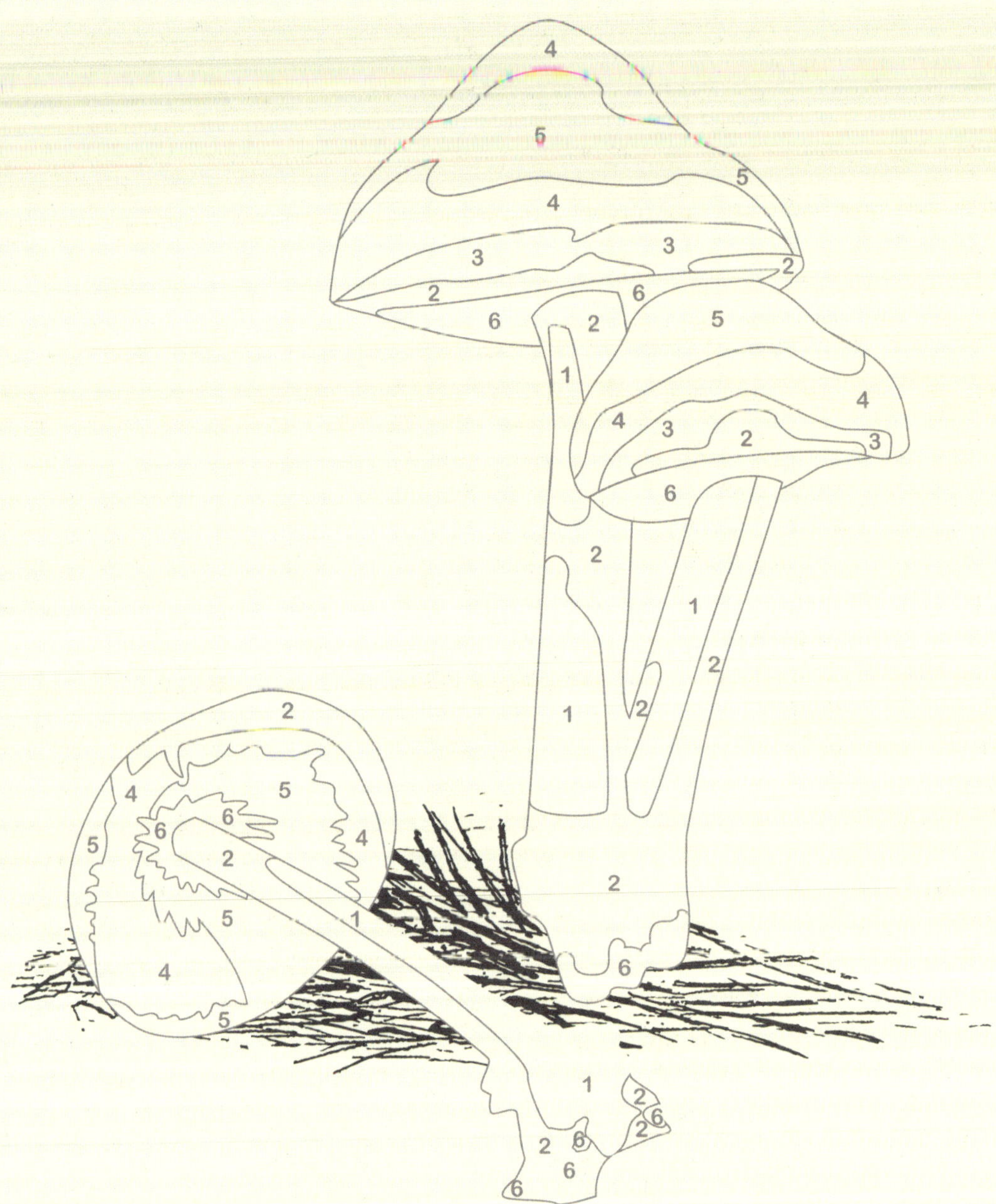

FLYING SAUCER

Psilocybe azurescens

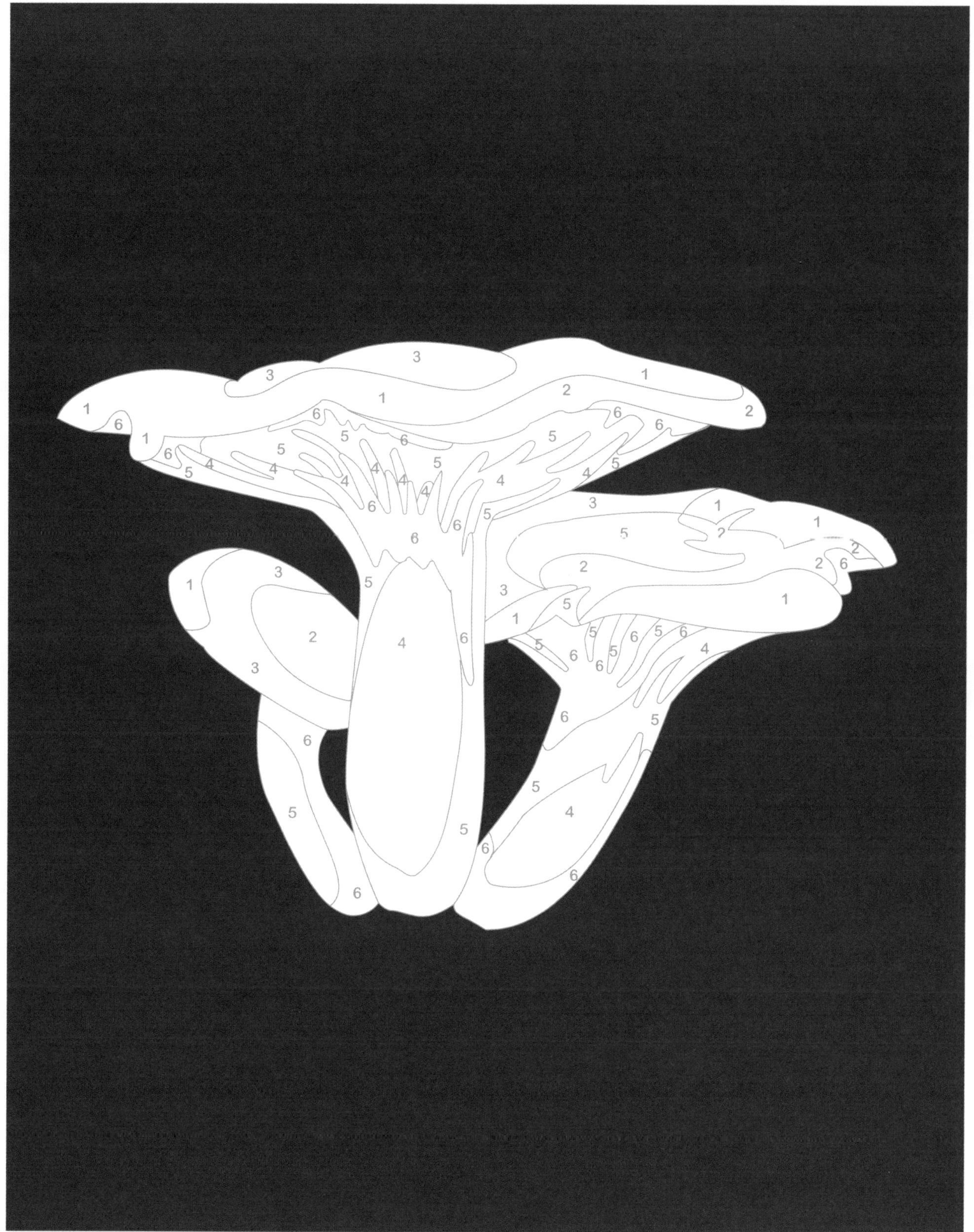

JACK-O'-LANTERN MUSHROOM

Omphalotus olearius

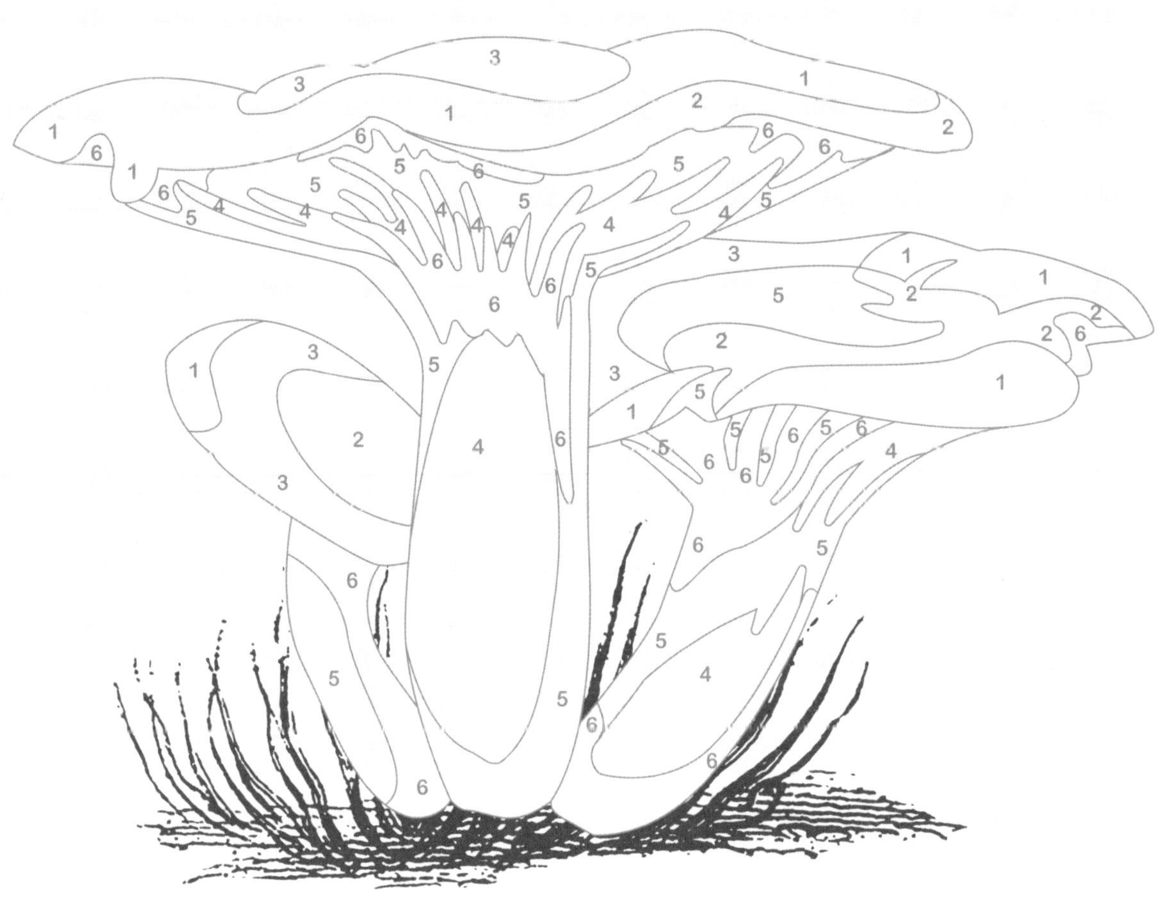

JACK-O'-LANTERN MUSHROOM

Omphalotus olearius

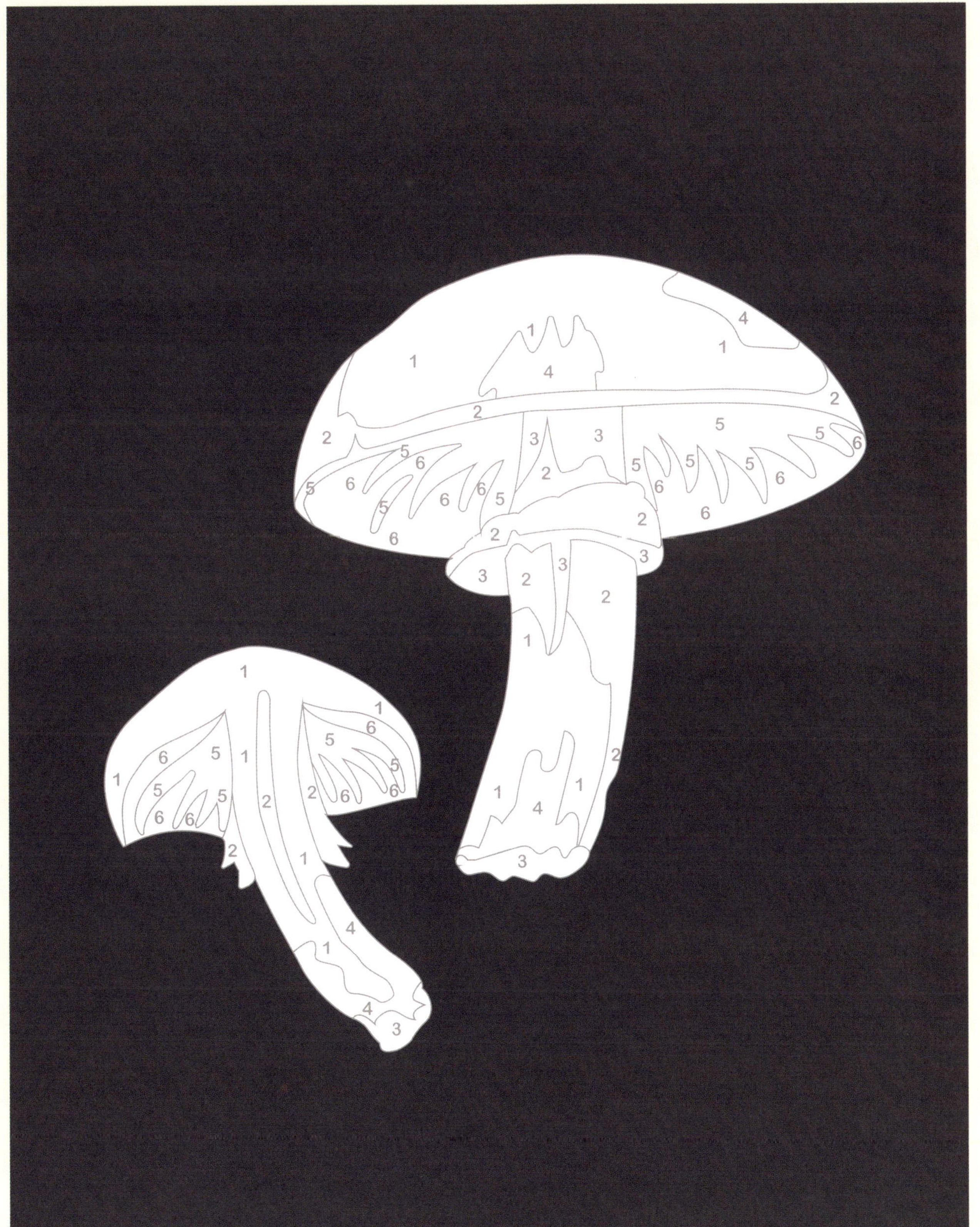

YELLOW STAINER

Agaricus xanthodermus

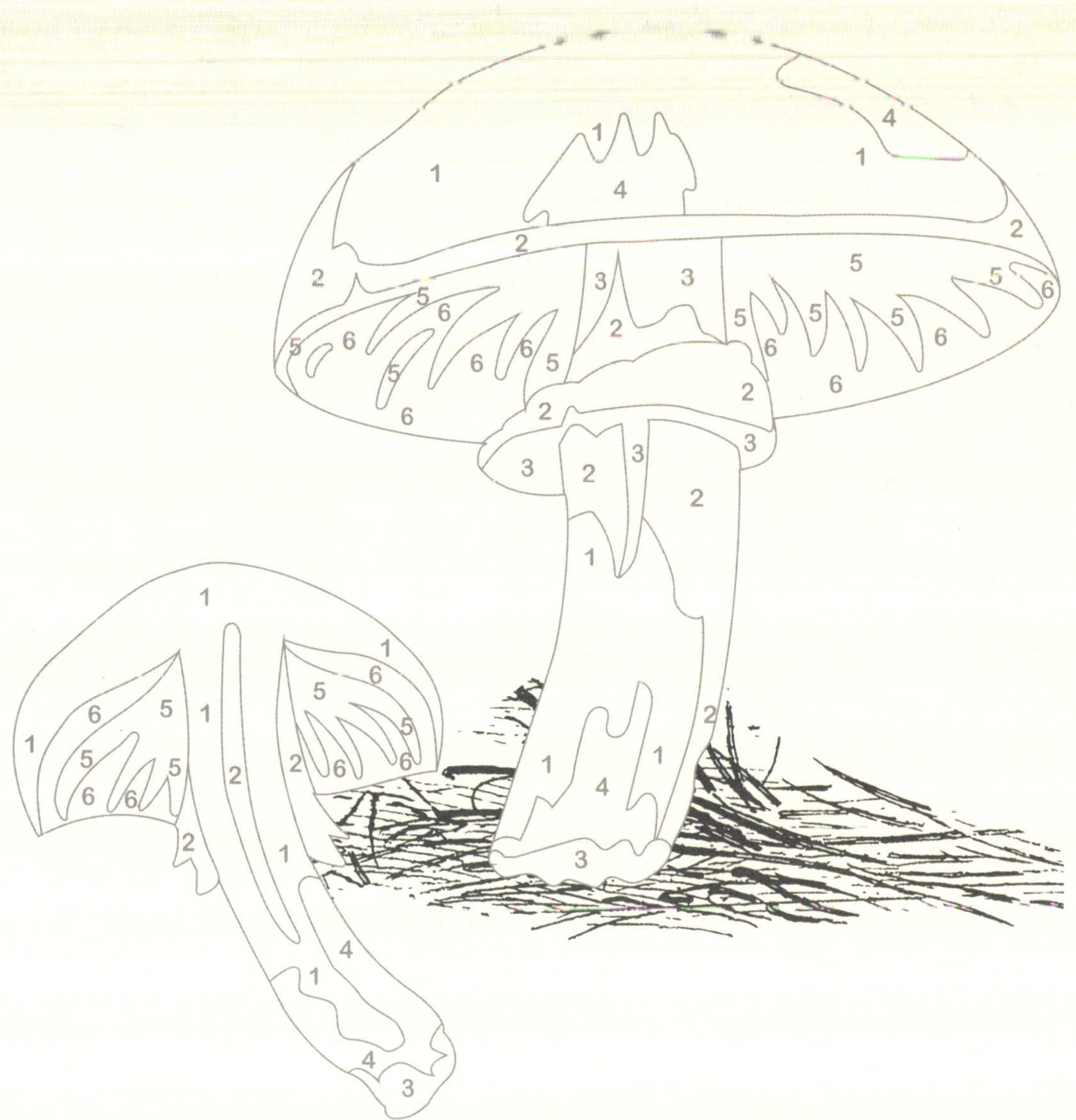

YELLOW STAINER

Agaricus xanthodermus

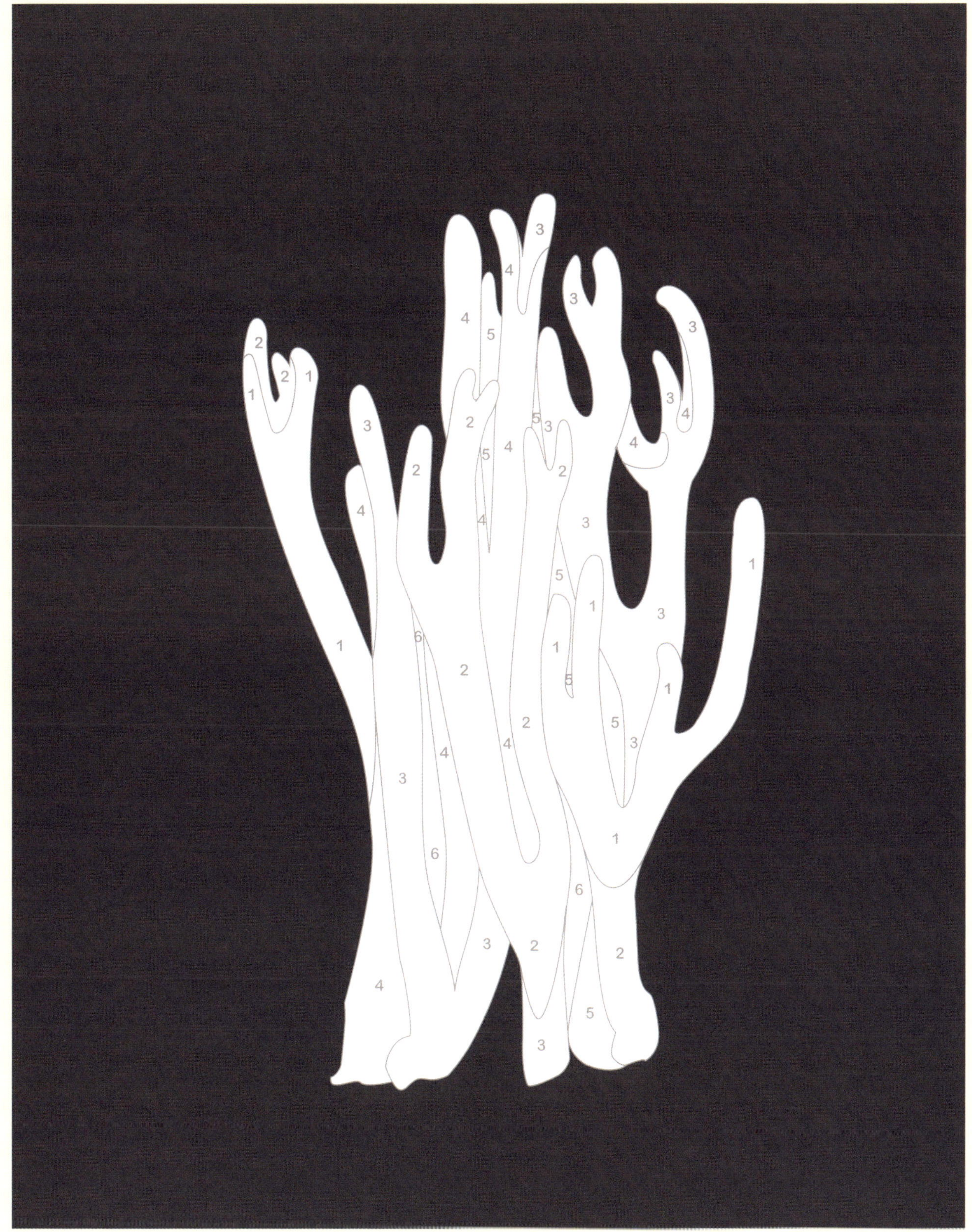

VIOLET CORAL

Clavaria zollingeri

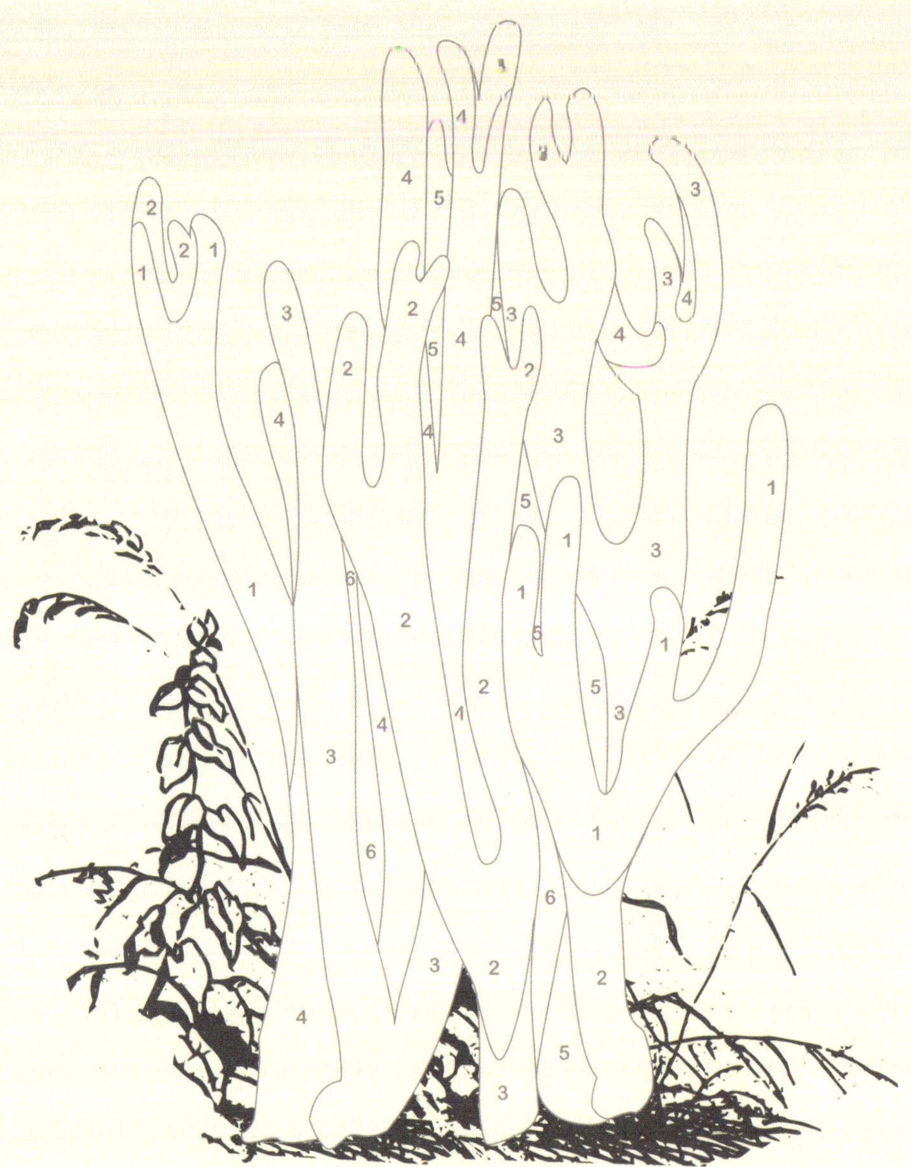

VIOLET CORAL

Clavaria zollingeri

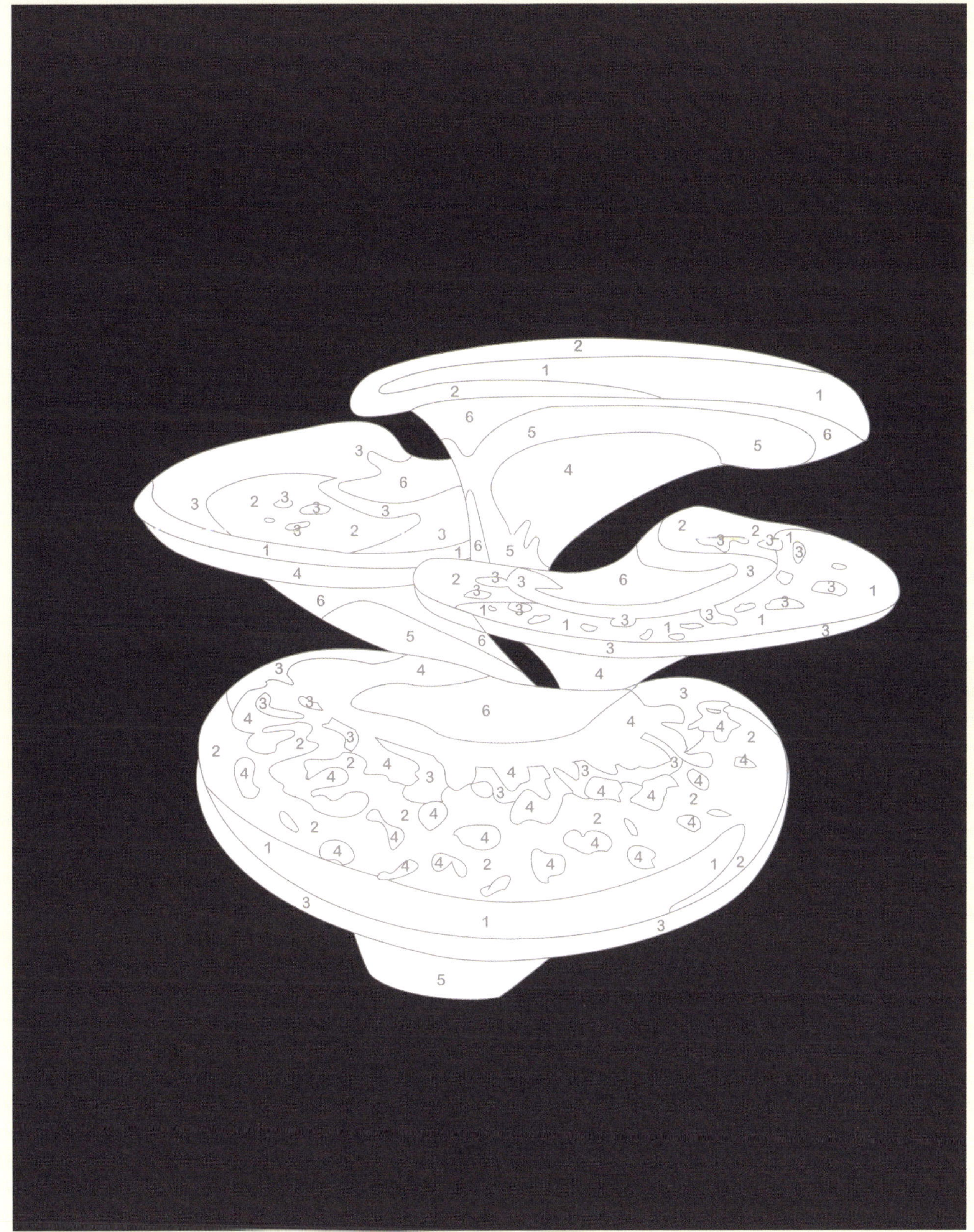

DRYAD'S SADDLE

Polyporus squamosus

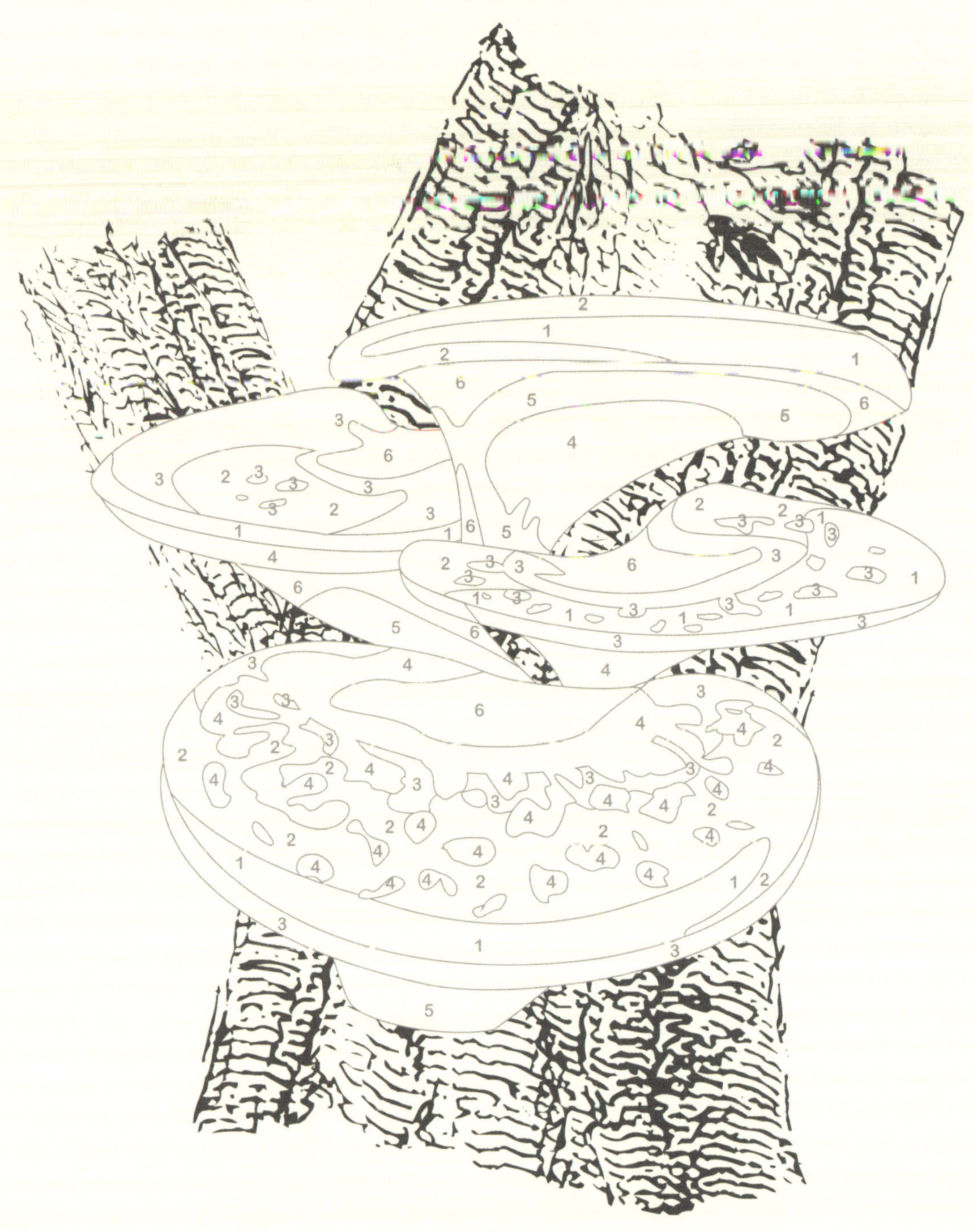

DRYAD'S SADDLE

Polyporus squamosus

PAINT SWATCH KEY

Place a drop of your mixed paint next to each swatch for your selected image to ensure you have a match before you begin painting (see page 11 for instructions).

FIG. 01 FLY AGARIC

1
15 Titanium White
4 Unbleached Titanium
1 Neutral Gray 5

2
5 Titanium White
4 Unbleached Titanium
1 Neutral Gray 5

3
4 Unbleached Titanium
3 Raw Umber

4
4 Cadmium Red Medium Hue
3 Light Pink
1 Brilliant Yellow Green
1 Naples Yellow Hue

5
7 Cadmium Red Medium Hue
4 Brilliant Yellow Green
2 Light Pink
1 Naples Yellow Hue

6
17 Ivory Black
6 Titanium White
5 Alizarin Crimson Hue Permanent
1 Brilliant Yellow Green
1 Neutral Gray 5

FIG. 02 ANISEED TOADSTOOL

1
30 Titanium White
5 Light Blue Permanent
2 Neutral Gray 5
2 Unbleached Titanium
1 Light Pink

2
5 Light Blue Permanent
5 Titanium White
2 Neutral Gray 5
2 Unbleached Titanium
1 Light Pink

3
5 Light Blue Permanent
4 Light Pink
4 Neutral Gray 5
2 Unbleached Titanium
3 Ivory Black
1 Turquoise Blue

4
25 Titanium White
6 Neutral Gray 5
1 Light Blue Permanent

5
9 Neutral Gray 5
9 Titanium White
1 Light Blue Permanent

6
10 Neutral Gray 5
1 Light Blue Permanent

FIG. 03 INKY CAP

1
20 Titanium White
2 Neutral Gray 5
2 Unbleached Titanium

2
15 Titanium White
3 Neutral Gray 5
2 Unbleached Titanium

3
10 Titanium White
4 Neutral Gray 5
3 Light Blue Violet
2 Unbleached Titanium
1 Brilliant Purple

4
3 Neutral Gray 5
3 Unbleached Titanium
2 Titanium White
1 Brilliant Purple

5
3 Ivory Black
2 Neutral Gray 5
1 Prism Violet
1 Titanium White
1 Ultramarine Blue

6
3 Ultramarine Blue
2 Neutral Gray 5
1 Mars Black
1 Prism Violet

1

20　Titanium White
3　Unbleached Titanium
1　Neutral Gray 5

2

15　Titanium White
4　Unbleached Titanium
1　Neutral Gray 5

3

5　Titanium White
4　Unbleached Titanium
1　Neutral Gray 5

4

4　Titanium White
4　Unbleached Titanium
2　Neutral Gray 5
1　Raw Sienna

5

7　Titanium White
1　Light Blue Permanent
1　Light Pink
1　Raw Sienna

6

7　Neutral Gray 5
3　Burnt Umber

1

15　Titanium White
4　Unbleached Titanium
1　Neutral Gray 5

2

5　Titanium White
4　Unbleached Titanium
1　Neutral Gray 5

3

8　Titanium White
6　Raw Sienna
5　Unbleached Titanium
2　Light Pink
1　Light Blue Permanent

4

3　Raw Sienna
3　Unbleached Titanium
1　Cadmium Orange Hue
1　Neutral Gray 5

5

1　Cadmium Orange Hue
1　Neutral Gray 5
1　Red Oxide
1　Unbleached Titanium

6

2　Red Oxide
1　Burnt Sienna
1　Burnt Umber
1　Ivory Black
1　Light Blue Permanent

1

15　Titanium White
3　Light Pink
3　Unbleached Titanium

2

25　Titanium White
5　Unbleached Titanium
2　Raw Sienna
1　Red Oxide

3

15　Titanium White
2　Raw Sienna
1　Red Oxide

4

5　Titanium White
3　Burnt Sienna
1　Burnt Umber
1　Light Pink

5

5　Burnt Sienna
2　Unbleached Titanium
1　Light Blue Permanent

6

5　Raw Umber
2　Ivory Black

FIG. 07

1
25 Titanium White
3 Neutral Gray 5
2 Light Pink
1 Brilliant Yellow Green
1 Light Green Permanent

2
25 Titanium White
15 Neutral Gray 5
2 Light Pink
1 Light Green Permanent

3
25 Neutral Gray 5
9 Titanium White
1 Light Green Permanent
1 Light Pink

4
2 Green Deep Permanent
2 Light Pink
2 Neutral Gray 5
1 Cerulean Blue Hue
1 Unbleached Titanium

5
2 Green Deep Permanent
2 Light Pink
2 Neutral Gray 5
1 Cerulean Blue Hue
1 Ivory Black
1 Unbleached Titanium

6
3 Green Deep Permanent
3 Ivory Black
2 Cerulean Blue Hue
2 Light Pink
2 Neutral Gray 5

FIG. 08

1
6 Light Pink
2 Titanium White
2 Yellow Oxide
1 Cadmium Orange Hue
1 Raw Sienna

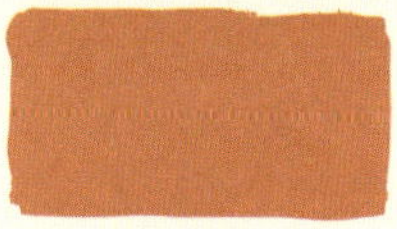

2
3 Raw Sienna
2 Light Pink
1 Cadmium Red Light Hue

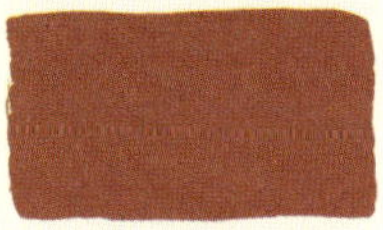

3
4 Titanium White
2 Raw Sienna
2 Red Oxide
2 Unbleached Titanium
1 Light Pink

4
3 Light Pink
2 Cadmium Red Light Hue
2 Raw Sienna
1 Cadmium Red Medium Hue
1 Red Oxide

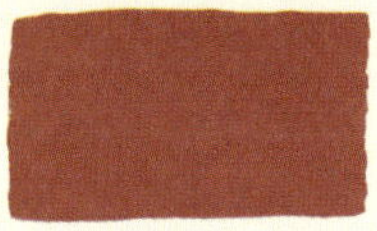

5
3 Light Pink
2 Red Oxide
1 Cadmium Red Deep Hue
1 Cadmium Red Light Hue

6
2 Cadmium Red Deep Hue
2 Light Pink
1 Alizarin Crimson Hue Permanent
1 Burnt Sienna
1 Ivory Black

FIG. 09

1
30 Titanium White
1 Neutral Gray 5
1 Unbleached Titanium

2
15 Titanium White
4 Unbleached Titanium
1 Neutral Gray 5

3
5 Titanium White
4 Unbleached Titanium
2 Neutral Gray 5

4
5 Unbleached Titanium
1 Burnt Umber
1 Titanium White

5
35 Titanium White
5 Unbleached Titanium
3 Neutral Gray 5
1 Light Blue Permanent

6
10 Titanium White
5 Neutral Gray 5
5 Unbleached Titanium
1 Light Blue Permanent

1

4 Cadmium Red Medium Hue
3 Light Pink
1 Brilliant Yellow Green
1 Naples Yellow Hue

2

7 Cadmium Red Medium Hue
4 Brilliant Yellow Green
2 Light Pink
1 Naples Yellow Hue

3

12 Alizarin Crimson Hue Permanent
5 Naphthol Crimson
2 Ivory Black
1 Brilliant Yellow Green
1 Red Oxide

4

35 Titanium White
4 Unbleached Titanium
2 Neutral Gray 5
1 Brilliant Yellow Green
1 Light Pink

5

10 Titanium White
4 Unbleached Titanium
3 Neutral Gray 5
2 Brilliant Yellow Green
1 Raw Sienna

6

8 Titanium White
5 Neutral Gray 5
3 Raw Sienna
2 Brilliant Yellow Green

1

32 Titanium White
2 Brilliant Purple
2 Unbleached Titanium
1 Neutral Gray 5

2

20 Titanium White
3 Neutral Gray 5
3 Unbleached Titanium
1 Brilliant Purple

3

4 Titanium White
3 Neutral Gray 5
3 Unbleached Titanium
1 Brilliant Purple

4

5 Neutral Gray 5
2 Brilliant Purple
2 Unbleached Titanium

5

5 Neutral Gray 5
2 Unbleached Titanium
1 Dioxazine Purple
1 Naples Yellow Hue

6

1 Dioxazine Purple
1 Ivory Black
1 Naples Yellow Hue

1

15 Titanium White
10 Unbleached Titanium
1 Neutral Gray 5

2

8 Unbleached Titanium
1 Neutral Gray 5
1 Raw Sienna

3

5 Unbleached Titanium
2 Burnt Sienna
2 Neutral Gray 5

4

6 Neutral Gray 5
2 Red Oxide
1 Brilliant Yellow Green

5

5 Neutral Gray 5
3 Raw Umber
1 Titanium White

6

5 Raw Umber
2 Ivory Black

1

8 Titanium White
2 Light Pink
2 Unbleached Titanium
1 Neutral Gray 5

2

5 Titanium White
2 Raw Sienna
2 Unbleached Titanium
1 Neutral Gray 5

3

5 Unbleached Titanium
1 Burnt Umber
1 Raw Sienna
1 Titanium White

4

3 Raw Sienna
2 Light Pink
1 Cadmium Red Light Hue

5

2 Cadmium Red Medium Hue
2 Neutral Gray 5
2 Titanium White
1 Red Oxide

6

4 Neutral Gray 5
2 Cadmium Red Deep Hue
1 Red Oxide

1

50 Titanium White
2 Neutral Gray 5
1 Cerulean Blue Hue

2

18 Titanium White
2 Neutral Gray 5
1 Cerulean Blue Hue

3

3 Cerulean Blue Hue
2 Neutral Gray 5
2 Titanium White

4

3 Cobalt Blue Hue
2 Neutral Gray 5
2 Titanium White
1 Ivory Black

5

3 Cobalt Blue Hue
1 Ivory Black
1 Titanium White

6

5 Cobalt Blue Hue
1 Mars Black

1

10 Unbleached Titanium
4 Neutral Gray 5
4 Ultramarine Blue
3 Ivory Black
1 Prism Violet

2

3 Ultramarine Blue
3 Unbleached Titanium
2 Neutral Gray 5
1 Mars Black
1 Prism Violet

3

3 Ultramarine Blue
1 Mars Black
1 Neutral Gray 5
1 Prism Violet

4

4 Neutral Gray 5
2 Titanium White
1 Unbleached Titanium

5

15 Neutral Gray 5
3 Titanium White
1 Burnt Umber
1 Light Blue Permanent

6

15 Neutral Gray 5
3 Ivory Black
2 Light Blue Permanent
1 Burnt Umber

FIG. 16 FLYING SAUCER

1
10 Titanium White
4 Unbleached Titanium
2 Neutral Gray 5

2
5 Titanium White
4 Unbleached Titanium
2 Neutral Gray 5

3
25 Titanium White
5 Unbleached Titanium
2 Raw Sienna
1 Red Oxide

4
15 Titanium White
2 Raw Sienna
1 Red Oxide

5
5 Titanium White
3 Burnt Sienna
1 Light Pink
1 Raw Umber

6
5 Titanium White
3 Burnt Umber
1 Light Pink
1 Raw Sienna

FIG. 17 JACK-O'-LANTERN MUSHROOM

1
3 Naples Yellow Hue
1 Cadmium Yellow Deep Hue
1 Neutral Gray 5
1 Raw Sienna
1 Titanium White

2
3 Naples Yellow Hue
2 Cadmium Yellow Deep Hue
1 Neutral Gray 5
1 Raw Sienna

3
3 Naples Yellow Hue
3 Neutral Gray 5
2 Raw Sienna
1 Raw Umber

4
6 Neutral Gray 5
2 Red Oxide
1 Brilliant Yellow Green

5
6 Burnt Sienna
2 Neutral Gray 5
1 Brilliant Yellow Green
1 Light Pink
1 Raw Umber

6
3 Burnt Sienna
2 Burnt Umber
1 Brilliant Yellow Green
1 Raw Umber

FIG. 18 YELLOW STAINER

1
15 Titanium White
4 Unbleached Titanium
1 Neutral Gray 5

2
5 Titanium White
4 Unbleached Titanium
2 Neutral Gray 5

3
5 Neutral Gray 5
5 Titanium White
1 Raw Umber

4
2 Titanium White
1 Naples Yellow Hue

5
2 Red Oxide
1 Burnt Sienna
1 Burnt Umber
1 Ivory Black
1 Light Blue Permanent

6
4 Light Pink
1 Neutral Gray 5

1

3 Brilliant Purple
3 Titanium White
1 Naples Yellow Hue
1 Neutral Gray 5

2

4 Neutral Gray 5
3 Brilliant Purple
2 Titanium White
1 Deep Violet

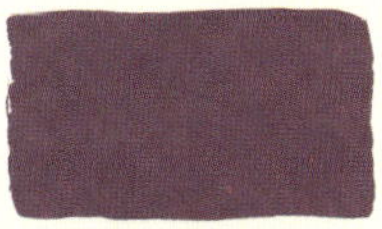

3

2 Brilliant Purple
2 Deep Violet
2 Neutral Gray 5
1 Titanium White

4

3 Ivory Black
1 Dioxazine Purple
1 Neutral Gray 5
1 Unbleached Titanium

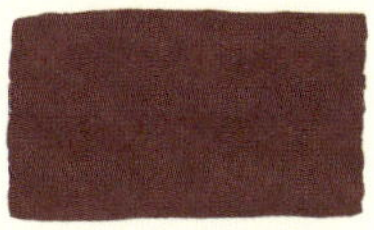

5

6 Alizarin Crimson Hue Permanent
4 Burnt Umber
3 Ivory Black
3 Neutral Gray 5

6

10 Ivory Black
5 Deep Violet
2 Alizarin Crimson Hue Permanent
1 Primary Yellow

1

10 Titanium White
4 Unbleached Titanium
2 Neutral Gray 5

2

8 Unbleached Titanium
5 Titanium White
4 Neutral Gray 5
1 Raw Umber

3

5 Titanium White
4 Unbleached Titanium
2 Neutral Gray 5

4

2 Burnt Umber
2 Raw Sienna
2 Titanium White
1 Light Blue Permanent

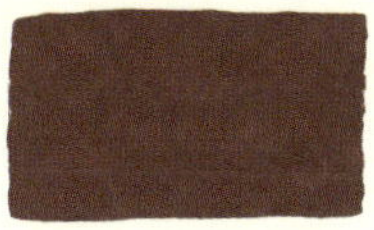

5

2 Burnt Umber
1 Neutral Gray 5

6

3 Raw Umber
2 Ivory Black
1 Burnt Umber
1 Neutral Gray 5

ABOUT COLOREADY AND
THE CREATORS OF THIS BOOK

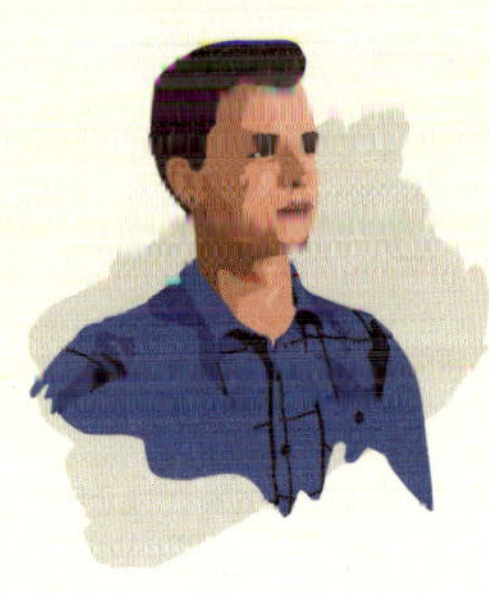

David Trawin is the creative force behind Coloready. He's been making stuff for as long as he remembers—from fake IDs at the age of eight to his teen years making punk zines with a handful of fellow creative misfits. Those zines took him to art school, where he majored in graphic design, then into his career, where he's worked for 20 years creating everything from T-shirts for a comedy brand (Buzz Aldrin wears the "Finders Keepers" astronaut-on-the-moon shirt he designed!) to alcohol graphics and tech products.

Coloready was born out of a love of graphic design, vintage hunting, and the immersive power of designing interior spaces. He currently resides in New Jersey with his wife (who cowrote this book), son, Olli, and daughter, Basil.

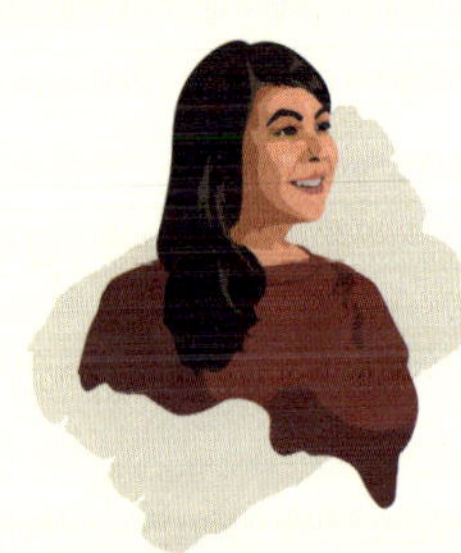

A. K. Roxas is a writer, editor, and internet media junkie. She's been writing stories and poetry her entire life, and so far has edited three books and contributed writing to two. But this is the first book she's gotten to help conceive and write from beginning to end. She also went to art school, but her art school is better than Dave's. She's spent her career focused on women's media, producing lifestyle and news pieces on finance, health, parenting, and weddings. She lives in New Jersey but dreams of owning a cozy shack by the beach.